first
names

MALALA
Yousafzai

Lisa Williamson

Illustrations by Mike Smith

Abrams Books for Young Readers
NEW YORK

All the facts in *First Names: Malala Yousafzai* have been carefully checked and are accurate to the best of our knowledge. Many of the stories rely on people's memories and news reports, and sometimes it's impossible to separate the truth from the legend, but we have brought Malala to life as faithfully as we can. Some of the passages in this book are actual quotes from Malala and other important people. You'll be able to tell which ones they are by the style of the type: *One child, one teacher, one book, and one pen can change the world.*

Library of Congress Control Number 2019947600

ISBN 978-1-4197-4074-9

Text copyright © 2020 Lisa Williamson
Illustrations copyright © 2020 Mike Smith
Book design by Charice Silverman

2019 © as U.K. edition. First published in 2019
by David Fickling Books Limited

Printed and bound in U.S.A.
10 9 8 7 6 5 4 3 2 1

Abrams Books for Young Readers are available at special discounts when
purchased in quantity for premiums and promotions as well as fundraising
or educational use. Special editions can also be created to specification. For
details, contact specialsales@abramsbooks.com or the address below.

Abrams® is a registered trademark of Harry N. Abrams, Inc.

ABRAMS The Art of Books
195 Broadway, New York, NY 10007
abramsbooks.com

Contents

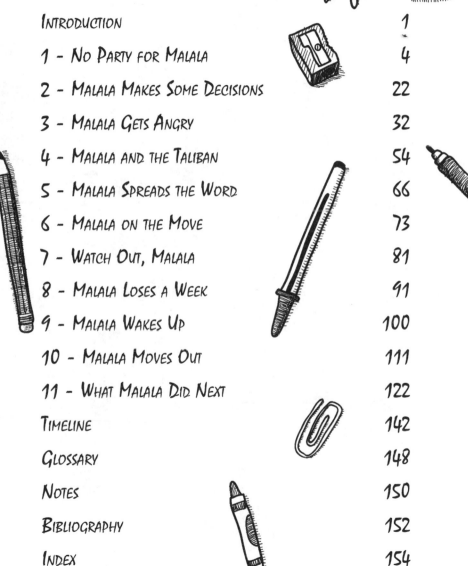

Introduction

October 9, 2012
Mingora, Swat Valley, Pakistan

Malala was in a good mood traveling home from school. She was pretty sure she'd aced the test that morning and was looking forward to a relaxing afternoon at home.

She was laughing with her best friend, Moniba, when **the school bus stopped suddenly**. A young man was standing in the road. He wore long white robes and a baseball cap.

"Is this the Khushal School bus?" he asked.

Another young man jumped onto the back of the bus. A hush fell over the girls as both men glared at them. Heart hammering in her chest, Malala found Moniba's hand and gave it a squeeze. Around twenty girls were crammed onto the hard plastic benches and they stared back, stunned, as the men scanned the bus.

"Who is Malala?" the second man asked gruffly. No one answered, but a few of the girls glanced in Malala's direction before they could stop themselves. Then the same man **raised a pistol**.

Malala froze with fear.

The man fixed his gaze on her and aimed his pistol at her head. The other girls began to scream, but Malala didn't make a sound. She just squeezed Moniba's hand harder.

A split second later, the man pulled the trigger and **everything went black**.

Malala was bleeding pro-
fusely as the bus swerved
through the heaving
streets of Mingora,
speeding toward the
local hospital. Once
there, doctors said her
prospects were grim, so grim that with a heavy heart, Malala's dad **began making funeral arrangements**. For a short while it looked like the men had succeeded in their quest to silence her.

But Malala did not die; she survived, and within days of her shooting she had become one of most famous teenagers on the planet. And she was more determined than ever to stand up for what she believed in: that every single girl in the world deserved to go to school. And she wanted as many people to hear her message as possible. She has since written books, appeared on television, and met all sorts of important people, including President Obama and the Queen of England. She's also the youngest person ever to win the Nobel Peace Prize.

Incredible stuff, right?

> Yes, but I'm actually quite ordinary, you know.

Yeah, right! Didn't Beyoncé wish you a happy birthday once?

> Well, yes . . .

And Selena Gomez called you her "role model!"

> OK, OK, but I promise you the real Malala isn't all that different from other girls.

Really?

> Yes! I love television, and I argue with my brothers over stupid things, like the TV remote and who ate the last slice of pizza!

You like pizza?

> Oh yes! And curry. And cupcakes. Mmmmm, especially cupcakes . . . And I like reading and listening to music and shopping and hanging out with my friends. Oh, and I hate getting up in the morning!

Hmm, all of that does sound pretty ordinary, actually.

So what makes Malala's story so special? Well, it didn't start with the shooting and the sudden fame. This ordinary girl was destined to achieve **extraordinary things** from the very moment she was born.

1 No Party for Malala

Ziauddin Yousafzai was over the moon. On the hot sticky morning of July 12, 1997 his wife gave birth to their first child—a beautiful bouncing baby girl. Over the next few days, he was so excited that he told everyone he met about the new addition to his family. People were polite but confused.

Why was he so happy and proud? After all, his wife had **a baby girl**. The thing is, in Pakistan, even today, from the second they enter the world, boys and girls are mostly treated very differently. When a baby boy is born, the family celebrates. Guns are fired up into the sky and visitors come to coo over the cradle and cram it with sweets and money. But when a baby girl is born . . . no gunshots, no gifts—people don't even bother to visit! Instead they sympathize with the "poor" mother and hope, for her sake, that her next child will be a boy.

Girls play as important a role in Pakistan as they do anywhere else in the world, but some families see raising girls as **a financial burden**. Girls aren't allowed to go out to work and provide for their families like boys do, and it can cost over a million rupees (about $15,000) to marry a daughter off.

Most girls spend their lives at home being wives and mothers, cooking and looking after the house and their children. And for some reason, that doesn't seem as important as earning a regular income. This is the way it's been for hundreds of years, which is why Ziauddin's celebrating his daughter was so unusual.

That's my dad for you! With a different set of parents, I'd probably be married with at least two babies by now.

To get to know me, you need to understand them first . . .

High-Flying Ziauddin

Ziauddin had a habit of challenging tradition that started when he was a boy—**and brother to five sisters**! While he and his older brother went off to school, the girls stayed at home and learned how to run a house, so that when they got married and had families of their own, they'd know what to do. Ziauddin thought this seemed **really unfair**, and as soon as he was old enough, he planned to do something about it.

But my dad had a really bad stutter, which made speaking in public unbelievably scary.

In spite of his stutter, Ziauddin entered a public speaking competition. He practiced and practiced and practiced until he knew his speech so well he could recite it in his sleep.

When the day of the competition rolled around, Ziauddin was terrified.

A-hem . . .

But then he spoke, and **something amazing happened**: his anxiety melted away and he made it to the end of his speech without stuttering once.

After that, there was no stopping him. Ziauddin's dad saw a great future ahead for his son, but it wasn't the future Ziauddin had planned for himself.

If Ziauddin didn't want to be a doctor, his dad wasn't going to pay his living expenses. That meant Ziauddin **couldn't afford college**.

In the end Ziauddin did make it to college thanks to a family friend named Akbar Khan. Akbar noticed the boy's eloquence and admired his vision. He insisted on lending him the money. **Ziauddin was thrilled**. It felt like his life was finally beginning! It also happened to be an interesting time in Pakistani history . . .

We can't let that brain of yours go to waste!

The election happened during Ziauddin's first term at college. Lots of student organizations that had been banned under the previous government were suddenly active again. **Everyone was feeling optimistic**.

With his experience of public speaking Ziauddin was a natural leader, and soon he was making speeches, chairing debates, and leading demonstrations all over the campus. And he became more dedicated than ever to his dream of opening a school.

Can't you get a smaller sign? I can't see a thing!

Politically, Pakistan had been on a bit of a rollercoaster for years, but just as my dad headed off to college in 1988, things were getting particularly exciting . . .

As part of India, Pakistan had been ruled by the British for over 90 years.

In 1947, we finally gained our independence. Two separate countries were formed: India, with a mainly Hindu population, and Pakistan, with a mainly Muslim population. Thirteen million people were forced to move, and one million were killed in terrible riots.

Our new country would be a democracy, represented by politicians who we, the people, elected—hooray! Except the military took control instead, and those elections didn't happen for twenty-three years!

Even then, the military wasn't happy to hand it over, and in 1971 there was a war in which hundreds of thousands of people died. The war led to a new country, Bangladesh, being formed.

Two years later, Zulfikar Ali Bhutto of the Pakistan People's Party (PPP) finally became Pakistan's first properly elected leader.

But the military was still lurking in the background, and in 1977 they ousted Bhutto and put their own General Zia in his place.

Horrifically, Bhutto was hanged by the military in 1979, even though important people from all over the world protested against it.

This is what really happened . . .

Whatever . . .

Zia brought in strict rules and religious laws: he banned nightclubs and horse racing, severely restricted women's roles in sport and performing arts, and in court, a woman's testimony was only given half as much importance as a man's!

In 1988, the year my dad became a student, Zia died in a plane crash and democracy finally seemed to be a possibility. *That's* why things seemed so exciting.

Ali Bhutto's daughter was leading her father's party in that year's elections, and she was very popular. Benazir Bhutto wanted change; she wanted women and men to be more equal, and she wanted better relations between Pakistan and India.

Freedom and liberty . . .

The PPP won and Benazir became the first female prime minister of Pakistan—and the first ever in the Islamic world.

She'd have won my vote!

TOOR PEKAI'S FIRST (AND LAST) DAY AT SCHOOL

Life couldn't have been more different for Malala's mom! Toor Pekai grew up in the same cluster of villages as Ziauddin, but the two of them didn't meet until they were much older.

When she was six, Toor Pekai's dad did something rather unusual: he sent her to school—and Toor Pekai really didn't appreciate it. She was the only girl in her class and she stuck out like a sore thumb. She spent most of the day wondering what her female cousins were up to and which games she was missing out on.

After her lessons were over, instead of going home, she went to the market and **swapped her school books for sweets**.

She worried that her dad might be angry at her, but no one said a word. The next day she went back to playing with her cousins in the fields and never set foot inside the school again.

It was only when she met my dad that Mom realized what she'd missed.

ZIAUDDIN MAKES A MOVE

In Pakistan, most marriages are arranged by the bride's and groom's families. But Ziauddin and Toor Pekai **fell in love** all by themselves!

I told you they were different!

Even so, it wasn't easy. Ziauddin sent Toor Pekai love poems. But at that time she couldn't read, so she didn't have a clue what they said. She did admire him for trying, though.

Eventually, Ziauddin went to ask for permission to marry Toor Pekai. But their fathers knew each other—and they weren't friends. Neither one of them wanted the marriage, but Ziauddin wasn't about to give up. He asked . . .

and asked . . .

and asked.

No.

No.

Still no!

After nine long months, Toor Pekai's dad gave in.

Phew! I might never have been born!

Ziauddin and Toor Pekai were perfect for each other. They laughed all the time and were really happy together. In most Pakistani households, the men are in charge—just the idea of asking their wives before making an important decision seems ludicrous. But Ziauddin was having none of this. He ran every decision by Toor Pekai, and listened carefully to her advice on matters big and small. Today he still says it's **her strength** that holds the family together during difficult times.

ZIAUDDIN'S DREAM

A few years after leaving college, Ziauddin set about opening his own school—a private elementary school for boys and girls that would teach in English. He found a shabby old building on the banks of a particularly smelly river, **spent his life savings** repairing and repainting it, and went door-to-door to find his first pupils.

He named it the Khushal School after one of his heroes, Khushal Khan Khattak, a legendary poet and warrior from the 1600s. Ziauddin wanted his students to be brave warriors too, only their weapons would not be swords, but their **pens and brains**!

Toor Pekai was at his side the entire time, helping him get the building ready and offering advice on business matters. They lived in a two-room shack opposite the school and hoped it wouldn't be like that forever.

On the day of the opening in 1994, the school looked spotless. There was just one (rather large) problem. Ziauddin had **only managed to recruit three students**! Parents had enjoyed talking to him on their doorsteps and liked his ideas, but they thought his brand-new school was too risky—better to keep their kids where they were.

Ziauddin carried on as normal, but he was seriously worried. The school was expensive to run, and soon they were falling behind on the rent. In the end, Toor Pekai **sold her wedding bangles** and the school was able to stay open for a few months longer. Then came some unbelievably bad luck: flash floods struck the area, and the school building was severely damaged along with everything in it! But even when the books and equipment were covered with slimy stinking mud, Ziauddin wouldn't let go of his dream, especially now— there was a baby on the way . . .

That baby was me, by the way!

Strangely, when Malala arrived in July 1997, Ziauddin's luck began to change. The family moved into more comfortable rooms above the school (they'd cleaned off the mud by then). And as word spread that the Khushal School was a good one, with great teachers and an excellent philosophy, more and more students started to trickle through the doors. Soon after Malala was born, there were **one hundred students**, many of them women. Pakistani girls were finally getting the same education as their brothers—Ziauddin's dream was coming true.

MALALA EXPLAINS SCHOOLS IN PAKISTAN

Blackboard

This classroom is probably very different from yours. There was no money for fancy gadgets, like tablets or computers.

Chalk

Pencil and paper

⚙ Education is supposed to be free in Pakistan, but the government schools aren't always the best. So private schools, like my dad's, have become more popular.

⚙ Our school day starts at six or seven in the morning because we head home at lunchtime. Most of us learn math, science, English language, social studies, art, PE, Urdu (Pakistan's official language), and Islamic studies.

⚙ Most schools that the government runs are for just boys, or just girls, but private schools often teach both—though girls are far less likely to go to school, or complete their education. My dad's school is mixed in elementary school, then girls and boys learn separately from age eleven on. Lessons are all in English too—because it's a really useful language for students to learn.

⚙ Corporal (physical) punishment is very common in Pakistani schools . . .

Forgotten your homework again, Habib?

But the goat really did eat it, sir!

That was never going to happen in my dad's school.

Ziauddin had big plans for his daughter from the start. He named her Malala after Malalai of Maiwand, a brave teenage warrior who lived in the 1800s.

According to legend, Afghan soldiers were struggling in a battle with the British army. When their flagbearer was killed, Malalai took his place and sang to encourage the troops. The Afghan soldiers won, but Malalai was killed.

Today she's remembered as Afghanistan's greatest heroine.

Ziauddin hoped that his Malala would grow up to be just as brave and influential as her namesake. He gave Malala a head start by insisting on adding her name to the family tree. **This was a BIG deal.**

In the three hundred years since our family tree was started, mine was the only female name to be included.

Until that point, only male names had been recorded—no women were listed at all. In fact, in Pakistan, many women go their entire lives without ever seeing their names written down, never mind getting it written on something as important as a family tree.

ALONG COMES TROUBLE

With the school downstairs and home upstairs, Malala saw a lot of her parents, and for the first two years of her life she enjoyed their undivided attention. So **imagine her horror** when a brand-new baby brother, Khushal, arrived in 1999 and then another, Atal, came along four years after that.

Why, God? Why did you give me these brothers? I didn't ask for them!

You're lucky there are only two of us!

In Pakistan, many couples have seven or eight children at least, so the Yousafzai family was really quite small.

Malala's brothers drove her up the wall from the start. They were **noisy and mischievous** and always using her things without asking. They never stopped annoying her, but on the upside, it was a lot easier (and much more fun) to play cricket or tag with three instead of one. Malala had to admit she sort of loved them.

Ziauddin loved his three children equally, but he and Malala always had an **extra-special bond**. If his sons complained that Malala was getting all the attention, he would tease them . . .

Khushal, when Malala is prime minister, you can be her secretary!

No! **I** will be prime minister and Malala will be **my** secretary!

A BIT OF A NERD

When it came to learning, there was no way Malala was going to let her dad down. Before she could even talk, she'd toddle into the empty school classrooms and play teacher for hours on end. By the time she was old enough to go to school herself, she was desperate to learn everything there was to learn.

Her class was full of hardworking girls, though. Education was precious, for girls especially, so the **pupils always behaved themselves** and listened carefully when the teacher was speaking. The girls were so enthusiastic that one time, when they were older, they decorated their hands with henna tattoos showing mathematical equations and chemical formulas. These tattoos are traditionally for weddings and national holidays and usually feature pretty pictures of flowers and butterflies!

Some people assumed Malala was always top of the class because her dad was the principal, but, in truth, **she really is incredibly smart**. In any case, there definitely wasn't any favoritism—Malala had to fight for the top spot every time!

In 2006, whcn Malala was about nine, a new girl arrived at the school, called Malka-e-Noor. She was naturally bright, like Malala, and so hardworking that one year she beat Malala and rose to the top of the class. When Malka-e-Noor was presented with the shiny trophy that Malala usually won, Malala was devastated. She managed to keep it together until she got home from school, but then she burst into tears. **Her dad was not sympathetic** . . .

Malala was even rivals with her best friend, Moniba. They'd known each other since they were toddlers, and they shared everything—from their deepest secrets, to face creams, to Justin Bieber lyrics . . . But that didn't stop them arguing all the time.

2   MALALA MAKES SOME DECISIONS

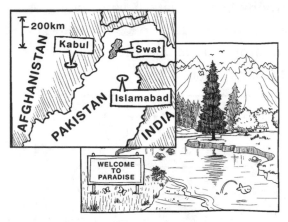

Paradise was a good description for the Swat Valley, the area of Pakistan where Malala grew up. Swat was called the Switzerland of Asia because of its snow-capped mountains and sparkling lakes. **Malala adored living there.** Although her home was in Mingora, a small city nestled deep in the valley, she was surrounded by countryside—she could see the mountains from her rooftop and smell the figs and peaches and apricots growing in the nearby orchards.

Any time she wasn't at school, or doing her homework, Malala was outside, running around with her brothers and the other kids in the neighborhood. They'd fly kites from the roof and play cricket and hopscotch in the alleyways. A short distance away there were some ancient ruins that were better than any playground. Malala and her friends would play hide-and-seek there for hours.

Sometimes, though, Malala liked to sneak away from the games and listen in on the grown-ups. The women would gather on the veranda to chat and joke, while the men sat inside and talked about politics and human rights. **It was the men's conversations** that really interested Malala. She didn't always understand what they were talking about, of course, but she could feel their passion . . .

> The Americans claim they've paid us billions to fight the group behind the 9/11 attacks.

> That's nonsense! We haven't seen a single cent!

> What are they talking about?

ONCE A PASHTUN, ALWAYS A PASHTUN

The men often talked about local politics too. Malala, her family, and most of the people who lived nearby were **Pashtuns and proud of it**. But Pashtuns living in some areas were suffering. After the 9/11 attacks on the World Trade Center and the Pentagon, some of the people responsible had taken refuge among Pashtun people, turning those areas into war zones.

MALALA EXPLAINS THE PASHTUN PEOPLE

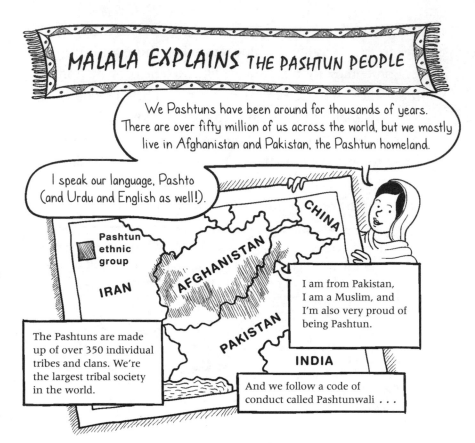

We Pashtuns have been around for thousands of years. There are over fifty million of us across the world, but we mostly live in Afghanistan and Pakistan, the Pashtun homeland.

I speak our language, Pashto (and Urdu and English as well!).

CHINA

Pashtun ethnic group

IRAN

AFGHANISTAN

I am from Pakistan, I am a Muslim, and I'm also very proud of being Pashtun.

PAKISTAN

The Pashtuns are made up of over 350 individual tribes and clans. We're the largest tribal society in the world.

INDIA

And we follow a code of conduct called Pashtunwali . . .

Melmastia (hospitality)—All Pashtuns must show hospitality to every visitor.

Sabat (loyalty)—Pashtuns must always stand up for their friends, family, and fellow tribe members

Khegara/Shegara (righteousness)—Pashtuns must behave respectfully to people, animals, and the environment around them.

Pashtunwali—the not so good bits

Nyaw aw Badal (justice and revenge)—Pashtuns are supposed to seek revenge for any wrongdoing. There is no time limit, and if, for any reason, you can't reach the person who offended you, their closest male relation must suffer instead!

Life in the Mountains

Twice a year, Malala and her family left Mingora and took a bus high up into the mountains to Shangla, the district her parents came from. They still had extended family there, and Malala loved visiting them. There were **streams and waterfalls to explore**, countless cousins to play with, and, even though her aunts and uncles didn't have much money, there was always **plenty of delicious food to eat**—curries and rice and spinach and big fat slabs of cake.

As Malala got older, however, she started to notice that life in Shangla wasn't quite as perfect as she'd thought, especially for the women in the village:

⚙ They weren't allowed to stop and chat with a man unless he was a close relative.

⚙ They certainly weren't encouraged to learn to read or write.

⚙ And most of them observed purdah, which meant they had to hide their faces when they left the house . . .

MALALA EXPLAINS PURDAH

- Purdah literally means veil or screen, and in Pakistan, Muslim women are observing Purdah when they cover their face or sometimes their whole body in public and live in purdah quarters—separate from the men—at home.

- The idea of purdah comes from the Holy Qur'an, the book that teaches Muslims about Islam. Verse 24:31 says that women *"shall not reveal any parts of their bodies, except that which is necessary outside of the home."*

- Purdah can be different for women in different countries and communities.

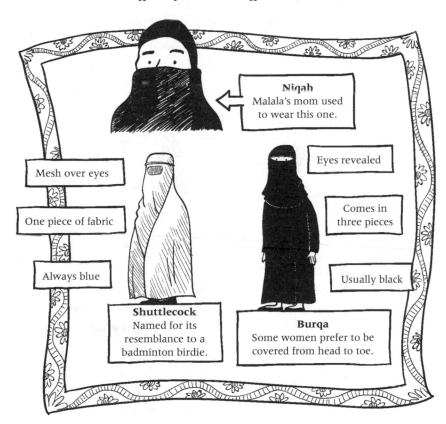

Niqab
Malala's mom used to wear this one.

Mesh over eyes

One piece of fabric

Always blue

Shuttlecock
Named for its resemblance to a badminton birdie.

Eyes revealed

Comes in three pieces

Usually black

Burqa
Some women prefer to be covered from head to toe.

⚙ **There are different ways of looking at Purdah.**

Huh, it's just a way of controlling women.

Actually, I like it. Men can't judge me by my looks; they have to get to know me.

If a woman wants to observe purdah, that's her choice, but it's not for me. My face is my identity!

The women in the village also weren't allowed any kind of education. While Toor Pekai was eager for her daughter to learn, all of Malala's female cousins stayed at home. Malala was desperate to know why, and so she asked her uncles . . .

Sending girls to school is a BIG waste of time!

Malala loved and respected her uncles, but their answers horrified her. She desperately wanted to convince them that they were wrong, but she didn't dare. If a boy talked back to an older family member, it was considered rude. **But if a girl did it?** Well, that was unheard of!

Malala bit her tongue and complained to her dad later. Ziauddin agreed with her, and promised he would never force her to do anything she didn't want to. He told her she would be "as free as a bird," but then he went on to explain that things were much worse just over the border in Afghanistan since a group called **the Taliban had taken over the country** . . .

They punish women for ridiculous things, like laughing in public, or wearing nail polish!

What!? Thank goodness I live in Swat.

MELMASTIA IN ACTION

Back in Mingora, with the school successful, the family had been able to move to a bigger house further away from the school. They weren't exactly rich, but, much to Malala's delight, **they could finally afford a TV!**

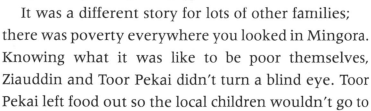

It was a different story for lots of other families; there was poverty everywhere you looked in Mingora. Knowing what it was like to be poor themselves, Ziauddin and Toor Pekai didn't turn a blind eye. Toor Pekai left food out so the local children wouldn't go to school with empty stomachs and Ziauddin was able to offer over **one hundred scholarships** to students who couldn't afford the fees. They both took their Pashtun hospitality very seriously, so Malala's house was always packed with people who needed their help. Sometimes it was so busy that Ziauddin joked it felt more like a boarding house.

THE SCAVENGER KIDS

The new house wasn't particularly fancy, partly because of the garbage dump nearby, which stank, especially in the summer. Malala always avoided the dump if she could, but one sunny afternoon, when she was about eight, Toor Pekai sent her there to throw away some potato peels. Malala was holding her breath as the stench of rotting food grew stronger and stronger, when she noticed a girl of about her own age **picking through the trash** for anything she could sell—metal cans, bottle tops, shards of glass, or scraps of paper. The girl had matted hair and a dirty-smeared face, and she wasn't alone. Looking around, Malala noticed **dozens of children** scavenging.

Malala was horrified, but she also desperately

wanted to talk to the girl and ask how she had ended up there. But Malala was too scared.

When she went home, she begged her dad to offer the children scholarships. **With tears in his eyes**, he explained that the children's families would be relying on the few rupees their children earned each day from the scraps they collected. Even with a scholarship, these families couldn't afford to send their kids to school. Malala was so upset and frustrated by the unfairness of it all that **she couldn't sleep**.

Sanju's Magic Pencil

The next day, as usual, Malala raced home from school to watch TV. She was particularly obsessed with a show called *Shaka Laka Boom Boom*. It was about a boy named Sanju who owned a magic pencil that brought anything he drew to life. For years, Malala dreamed of having her own magic pencil, but that afternoon, as she watched Sanju magically work his way out of problem after problem, she just kept thinking about the girl from the dump. Suddenly, it dawned on Malala that magic wouldn't fix all the unfairness in the world. If she wanted things to change, there was only one way to do it . . .

I'll have to make it happen myself.

3 MALALA GETS ANGRY

One morning, in October 2005, eight-year-old Malala was sitting in class when her desk began to shake. She knew exactly what was happening.

Chairs scraped across the floor as students hurried to flee the trembling classroom. Out in the playground, the girls did as they'd been taught in the earthquake drills, but this was the real deal, and they couldn't help panicking. Some children fell over and a few started to cry. Malala managed to keep her cool, but she was definitely rattled.

Swat lies in a geographical fault zone and earthquakes had rumbled beneath them several times before, but somehow this one felt different—**bigger, louder, and much, much stronger**.

"Keep calm," a teacher barked. "It will be over soon."

At first it seemed she was right. The ground stopped shaking after a few minutes, the children caught their breath, blinked away their tears and headed back inside. But they'd barely picked up their pencils when the walls and desks began to shake all over again. This time, they were sent home for the day.

Aftershocks shook the ground all night long and Toor Pekai insisted the family stay outside—that way if the roof caved in it wouldn't bury them all in their beds. They huddled together in the courtyard and **stayed outside all night**, reciting verses from the Holy Qur'an to keep their spirits up. By morning they were all exhausted.

AFTERSHOCK

The earthquake was bad—**one of the worst** in Pakistan's history. It was a magnitude 7.6 quake—which is massive! In fact, people felt the rumblings as far away as Delhi in India and Kabul in Afghanistan.

The epicenter of the earthquake (near the city of Muzaffarabad) was only about 60 miles (100 kilometers) away, yet somehow Mingora had been more or less spared. So when the family gathered around the TV, **they were shocked** as the extent of the damage became clear. The numbers blew their minds . . .

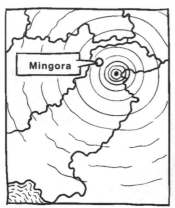

In less than twenty-four hours, over seventy-five thousand people have died, and eleven thousand children have been orphaned.

Malala and her family waited anxiously for news from their relatives up in the mountains, and when it came, it wasn't good. In Ziauddin's tiny village, **eight people had lost their lives**, including the four young daughters of the local cleric. Ziauddin set off immediately to see if he could help. Malala begged to go with him, but her dad said no way: it was far too dangerous.

The next few days crawled by. When Ziauddin finally returned, his report was grim. His brothers had watched with horror as rocks slid down the mountains toward them, crushing everything in their path. They'd thought **the world was coming to an end**. Many people in the Shangla district had lost their lives and thousands of buildings had been reduced to dust.

So many people were in dire need that the family sprang into action. They collected donations of food, clothes, blankets, and money, but it was nowhere near enough—the damage was just too widespread.

A WARNING FROM GOD?

Government help was a long time coming. Many of the worst-hit areas were difficult to reach because **roads and bridges had been destroyed** in the quake. But a religious group called Tehrik-e-Nifaz-e-Shariat-e-Mohammadi (TNSM for short) did get to the scene almost immediately, reaching corners of the country that might otherwise have been ignored. They helped to clear rubble and repair buildings, lead prayers, bury the dead, and take in many of the orphaned children.

Unfortunately, there was a catch. The TNSM had some rather unsettling ideas. They firmly believed that the earthquake was a warning from God, and they threatened worse was to come if the locals didn't change their ways. Malala knew that earthquakes could easily be explained by science and she assumed other people would think the same way.

Unfortunately, not everyone in Swat had the benefit of an education. A lot of people really were taken in by these words, including several members of Malala's own family. The TNSM knew that **fear could be a powerful tool**, and they were all set to use it to their own advantage—because, it turned out, they were actually linked to the Pakistani Taliban!

And it was the Taliban who punished women for laughing!

MALALA EXPLAINS THE TALIBAN

People first started to hear the name Taliban in 1994.

War broke out in Afghanistan in 1979, when the Soviet army (from the USSR) invaded. The Soviets were defeated in 1989, but the new Afghan government struggled to keep the peace between rival groups. In 1994, a group of mainly Pashtun men, calling themselves "Talibs," arrived promising to bring peace, and many Afghans welcomed them with open arms. For a while things really did get better.

We're glad that's over!

1989

The Soviet Union

AFGHANISTAN

IRAN

PAKISTAN

INDIA

But it turned out the Talibs had more than just peace on their minds.

These men had been educated in madrasas (traditional Islamic schools). There was nothing unusual about that, except the madrasas these men went to pushed extreme ideas.

MADRASAS

✿ Madrasas have been around since the tenth century. There are twenty-five thousand just in Pakistan today!

✿ Students of all ages, both girls and boys, can study at madrasas full-time or part-time. Madrasa students recite and interpret passages from the Holy Qur´an, as well as learning philosophy, theology, Arabic grammar, and Muslim history.

> I used to go to one myself after ordinary school.

✿ Madrasas are usually peaceful places, but there is evidence that a tiny number of them could be teaching extreme ideas to their students. Ideas that might encourage terrorism.

The Talibs wanted to bring in their own type of justice, using the Muslim Sharia law. But they interpreted the laws in a very extreme way, with harsh punishments.

> You took a girlfriend when you're already married—your punishment is death!

> So what do you get for stealing?

> You lose a hand!

Sharia Law

"Sharia" literally means "the path" or "a road that leads to water." Sharia is a sort of code for Muslims to show them how they should live their lives. But the laws can be interpreted differently from country to country, and even from person to person.

The Taliban would do anything to get what they wanted— destroying buildings, burning land, and killing anyone who got in their way.

Everything will be better with us in charge.

I don't trust these people!

The leaders were so persuasive that they managed to recruit thousands of ordinary Afghan Muslims who were desperate for change. Soon, the group was powerful enough to take charge of large parts of Afghanistan.

The Taliban were driven out of Afghanistan in 2001, but many of the leaders fled over the border into Pakistan, where small groups, like the TNSM, sprang up.

AFGHANISTAN IN 2001

▧ **Taliban-controlled areas**

These groups came together and formed the Tehrik-i-Taliban Pakistan—the Taliban Movement of Pakistan.

Radio Mullah

A few months after the quake, when Malala was nine, a new (illegal) radio station hit the airwaves. It was hosted by twenty-eight-year-old Maulana Fazlullah and broadcast twice a day. Fazlullah talked about the importance of daily prayer and interpreted sections of the Holy Qur'an. His nighttime show became especially popular with housewives, like Toor Pekai, who thought he **sounded wise and charismatic**. They loved the way he ordered male listeners out of the room so he could talk directly to women, promising them special rights under his new version of Sharia law.

But Fazlullah had a sneaky reason for trying to appeal to women. In Pakistan, without education, most women are illiterate, so they can't read newspapers for themselves. For a lot of them, Radio Mullah was **their only window to the outside world**, and Fazlullah knew it.

It's time for Radio Mullah.

Best part of the day!

Once he was sure he had won their trust, it only took a few months for his message to change. Suddenly, he was telling people what to wear and what they should and shouldn't be doing. Most worrying of all, his views sounded suspiciously like those of the Taliban.

Toor Pekai and her friends were terrified, even though Malala tried again and again to explain to them that the earthquake was not a punishment from God. Fazlullah was so convincing, he even had fans among educated people. Some teachers in the Khushal School supported him. **Ziauddin was appalled**. He couldn't understand what everyone saw in Fazlullah. The man claimed to be a great scholar when, in reality, he hadn't even finished high school.

The trouble was, a change in the Pakistani government system was desperately needed and Fazlullah had managed to convince many of his listeners that he was the man to fix their problems.

At school, Radio Mullah's fiery broadcasts were the talk of the playground. Malala hated it.

FAZLULLAH

✪ Fazlullah was married to the daughter of the leader of the TNSM. When her dad was imprisoned, in 2002, Fazlullah took his job. He read his father-in-law's books in an attempt to turn himself into an Islamic scholar.

✪ Fazullah encouraged his male followers to adopt his look, with long beards and black turbans. He was one of the first clerics to preach on the radio.

Too short!

✪ He knew many people had lost faith in the government, so he presented himself as a Robin Hood figure, bringing power and dignity back to ordinary Muslims. But after he won them over, he massively changed his tune.

✪ When the various extremist groups came together to form an alliance, Fazlullah shot up through the ranks to become the head of the Swat Taliban.

One day, Fazlullah said something that Malala just couldn't ignore.

Schools for girls are forbidden by Islam.

I was furious! What right did Fazlullah have to stop me and my friends from going to school?

She marched into class the following day, expecting her classmates to be just as furious as she was. Many of them were, but **most were just scared**.

After that, girls all over Swat started to drop out of school. They were "good Muslims" according to Fazlullah, and he gave them the "honor" of listing their names on his show. On the other hand, he said, girls who were still going to school made him deeply unhappy, and he insulted them by comparing them to cattle, calling them "buffaloes" and "sheep."

Over the next few months, Fazlullah's sermons became more and more extreme.

The situation got worse and worse. Fazlullah's followers began patrolling the streets, listening out for the sound of forbidden television sets. If they heard one, they'd then **burst into the owner's home** and smash the set to pieces!

People were so terrified that they started taking their TVs, DVDs and CDs to the town square to be burned in enormous bonfires.

But Malala's family defiantly held on to their own TV, though they kept it in a cupboard and only watched with the sound turned down.

Life was miserable, but when Fazlullah asked for help, people were only too eager to offer it. When he wanted to set up his own madrasa, his female fans showered him with money and gold. Some **even handed over their life savings**! Meanwhile, many men, fed up with a government that did nothing for its people, were inspired by Fazlullah's ambitious plans to take over and establish Sharia law. They volunteered in their droves to help build the madrasa, which Fazlullah planned to use as his headquarters.

Ghost Town

Mingora was changing, and not for the better. After everything he'd promised them, it soon became clear that Fazlullah's new rules would be **far worse for women than for men**. Then a huge banner appeared at the market, saying WOMEN NOT ALLOWED. The once bustling bazaar was suddenly empty, while Fazlullah's followers were now patrolling the streets in pickup trucks with machine guns mounted on their roofs.

At school, the seats in Malala's classroom were gradually starting to empty. Lessons carried on, but even some of Malala's teachers were now **refusing to teach girls**. And, with hardly any students in the school, Ziauddin wasn't earning much money.

As far as Malala was concerned, life had just about **hit rock-bottom**. So many people had been taken in by Fazlullah and his cronies . . .

I never knew—did they really believe what he said, or were they just terrified?

BLOODY SQUARE

Radio Mullah had been on air for about a year when Fazlullah's broadcast introduced a new feature. He started reading out the names of people who spoke out against the Taliban.

And this message goes out to Ali . . . how DARE you defy me!

The result was horrific! Many "offenders" were dragged to the town square where they were **flogged or killed**, their bodies dumped there as a warning to everyone. These people had only been saying what they thought—but to the Taliban this was a crime!

There was so much death and violence in the square that people renamed it Bloody Square.

Malala woke up every day feeling sick about what was going on in her beloved city. And things weren't about to get any better. One day, close to Malala's tenth birthday, Ziauddin discovered a note stuck to the school gates.

No prizes for guessing that it came from the Taliban.

Malala felt sick. But Ziauddin was determined not to give in to them. Defiantly, he had his reply published in the local newspaper.

Sir,
The school you are running is Western and infidel! You teach girls and you have a uniform that is un-Islamic. Stop this or you will be in trouble and your children will weep and cry for you.

'You can take my life,' says Ziauddin Yousafzai, 'but please don't kill my schoolchildren.'

The whole family were now **absolutely terrified** for Ziauddin—but Malala was also **incredibly impressed**. In a world where fear was king, her dad was standing up for what he believed in. She only hoped she would grow up to be even half as brave.

CHAOS IN THE CAPITAL

Just a couple of days after the Taliban left the note for Ziauddin, they set about attacking Swat's ancient monuments. In a few short weeks they blew up dozens of statues and tombs and plundered the museums and galleries, **wiping out thousands of years of history** in minutes.

They didn't stop there. As if they hadn't totally put tourists off visiting Swat already, they went on to blow up the ski lift and a hotel that catered to winter ski enthusiasts. They took over entire villages and police stations, plastering them with their black and white flag. Soon the police were **too afraid to do their jobs** and they began to leave the force in droves, announcing their resignations in the newspaper so the Taliban would know not to target them any more.

Having no police force in place and a disorganized local government was exactly how the Taliban liked it.

They could run things their way, and the people of Swat had no chance of fighting back.

It was like everyone was **under some kind of spell**! People had been so taken in by Fazlullah's lies it was almost impossible to change their minds. After all, Fazlullah had control of the radio waves and an army of followers. How could a ten-year-old girl and her schoolteacher-dad compete with that?

At home, without regular TV and only having a tiny courtyard to play in, **Malala was getting very bored**. Even board games had been banned!

Meanwhile, there was unrest all over Pakistan and chaos in the capital, Islamabad, which was usually quite calm and orderly. Although the Taliban hadn't reached the city, other extremist groups had. One group, based at the Red Mosque, in the center of the city, were plotting to overthrow the government and impose Sharia law. In July 2007, the army laid siege to the Red Mosque. The siege lasted eight days, and by the time it ended about one hundred people, from both sides, lay dead.

Even though he and the Taliban had nothing to do with it, Fazlullah used the bloodshed as an excuse to take things to the next level. On July 12, 2007 (Malala's tenth birthday), he took to the airwaves, and in a rage, officially declared war on the Pakistani government.

Happy birthday to me!

A Ray of Light

But all was not lost. There was still one person who might be able to help . . . one person brave enough to take on Fazlullah and the Taliban. She'd been out of the country for nine long years, but rumor had it **she was planning a comeback**, and she was going to campaign to become Pakistan's prime minister. Her name? Benazir Bhutto, the very politician who had inspired Ziauddin at college all those years ago. Malala was thrilled. She had grown up listening to Ziauddin talking about Benazir and she liked what she heard. Best of all, the one person who might be able to defeat the Taliban was a woman . . .

BENAZIR BHUTTO

⚙ Benazir had already been prime minister of Pakistan twice! This was before Malala was born, in the 1980s and 90s.

⚙ She'd taken over her dad's political party— the PPP—and vowed to continue his work.

I am not giving up!

⚙ People loved their female prime minister, and BIG crowds gathered when she appeared in public. The government, on the other hand, wasn't so keen on her. She wanted to tackle crime, poverty, and the cheating in politics; she fought for women's rights too, but they hardly allowed her to make any changes.

⚙ Amazingly, she did make some amazing things happen during her time in office: She appointed female judges, helped to create a women's bank, and opened an all-female police station.

When women were mostly hidden behind closed doors, this was a HUGE deal.

After losing the election back in 1997, Benazir had been accused of corruption and forced out of the country. Charges against her were finally dropped in 2007, and that October—three months after

51

Fazlullah had declared war on the government—
she returned to Pakistan to **a hero's welcome**. She
rode through the streets of Karachi on an open-top
bus and hundreds of thousands of cheering fans
turned up to welcome her. Millions of people living
without the influence of the Taliban watched the
coverage freely on TV, and over 900 miles (1,500
kilometers) away in Mingora, Malala and her
family huddled around their TV set in secret.

Led by General Musharraf and the military, the
government was very unpopular. **They had a terrible
reputation** for not looking after the human rights
of their people, discriminating in particular against
women and people who weren't Muslim. This made
it easy for groups like the Taliban to rise up. When

Benazir returned, there was hope that if she ran for government, she'd **win a massive victory** and make it her business to wipe out the likes of Fazlullah and the Taliban.

But the joy and excitement of her return didn't last long. Just a few hours into the parade, there was a massive explosion! The door of the bus was blown off, and its windows were shattered. But Benazir was resting in an armored compartment at the time, thank goodness! If it had happened minutes earlier, she'd have been caught up in the blast, which killed over 150 innocent people. It was **the biggest bomb ever** to go off in Pakistan.

The general public were devastated, even people who weren't huge fans of Benazir and her politics, and angry protests broke out across the country. People were furious that the government had not provided proper protection for Benazir and accusations were flying around about who might be responsible: the Taliban, Al-Qaeda (who carried out the 9/11 attacks in the United States), or even the government.

4 Malala and the Taliban

About a week after the bombing, the army rolled into Swat. The government had finally woken up to what the Taliban were doing there and so they sent in **three thousand soldiers** to push them out. Jeeps thundered through the streets and helicopters swarmed in the sky, dropping candy and tennis balls for the children below. Malala and her brothers tore through the alleyways near their house, competing to see **who could collect the most sweets**. With the army in town, surely Fazlullah and the Taliban wouldn't last much longer?

Yay! Sweets!

A few days later, a curfew was announced. Malala's family didn't know what that meant and had to ask their neighbors through a hole in the wall. They found out they were going to have to stay inside for the next twenty-four hours.

They soon understood why. That night, **Swat turned into a war zone** as the army attempted to drive the Taliban away. Malala's bedroom was flooded with white light, and the walls and ceiling shook as bomb blasts and gunfire echoed through the valley. Terrified, she leaped from her bed and spent the rest of the night huddled up with her parents and brothers, certain that at any minute the walls would collapse around them like a house of cards.

The next day, Mingora was eerily quiet. Ziauddin went out to investigate, and he came back with bad news. Despite everything the army had thrown at them, **the Taliban weren't backing down**. The curfew was extended and the army sent in more soldiers.

Over the next few weeks, Malala spent night after night curled up on her parents' bedroom floor (the bed was too small for all five of them!). Atal snored through all the noise, but Malala and Khushal struggled to sleep, so they tried to entertain themselves.

Sometimes, though, Malala just stuck her earplugs in and pretended she was somewhere else—a Pakistan where Fazlullah and the Taliban did not exist.

Disaster!

On November 24, 2007, Benazir Bhutto entered her nomination papers for the elections the following January. She'd just released details of her party's plans for the future and she wanted to focus on what she called the "Five Es"—employment, education, energy, environment, and equality. January seemed far away, but for Malala it was something to hope for.

On December 27, 2007, Malala and her family gathered around their TV (with the army in town they hoped it was safe to watch it openly again), as Benazir made a speech in Rawalpindi, a city just 90 miles (145 kilometers) south of Mingora. *"We will defeat the forces of extremism!"* Benazir insisted to loud roars of support.

The speech finished, she was waving to the jubilant crowds, and then **something awful happened**. There were gunshots and Benazir suddenly disappeared from view. A suicide bomber had blown himself up right next to the car Benazir was traveling in.

She died instantly.

Malala had seen it with her own eyes. She felt numb with shock. Benazir had been their one great hope, and just like that, **she was gone**.

Pashtun code strictly forbade any sort of violence against women, but the Taliban had attacked Benazir in public! The entire nation was shocked. Were there no limits to the Taliban's evil? All around her people were weeping and wailing, but Malala was thinking hard. She'd had enough of being scared. She might only be ten years old, but she vowed to herself that **she would rise up against the darkness** that had killed Benazir.

Keep Calm and Carry On

Malala did her best to carry on as normal, which is easier said than done when army helicopters frequently hovered over her school, drowning out the teachers' voices.

I'm going to stand up for what I believe in, no matter what the risk.

Malala was eleven, and the army and Taliban had been fighting for over a year and a half. Along with Moniba, she'd moved up to

the Khushal middle school and loved her new classes: algebra, chemistry and physics. **She was even daring to dream** that she might become a doctor or an inventor one day.

But it was around this time that Malala heard some sickening news. An elementary school in a town called Matta had been blown to smithereens and Fazlullah and his men were claiming responsibility.

No one had been hurt, thank goodness, but more and more schools were being targeted. Although the Taliban weren't patrolling the streets anymore, the army was still no match for them, and they still had a huge influence in Swat. Before long, **they'd hit over four hundred schools** across the region. The message was coming across loud and clear—they were only attacking schools that took girls. After her dad's piece in the paper, Malala felt sure their school must be on the Taliban's list. When she asked her dad why they were so against girls' education, he gave her an unexpected answer: he said **the Taliban were afraid of pens**! He meant that educating people gives them power, the power to question, to challenge things and to stand up for what they believe in.

Women made up around 50 percent of the population, and a huge number of them were not educated. Without education, Fazlullah had been able to manipulate so many of them; with education his deceptive tricks might not work so well.

Malala Gets Her Chance

For a while, Malala barely saw her dad because he was so busy attending meetings or speaking to the media. Unable to rely on the local government to stand up for the people, a few brave men had banded together to set up the Swat Qaumi Jirga, an assembly to challenge Fazlullah. Ziauddin had volunteered to be their spokesperson. *"If you stay silent you lose your right to exist,"* he told Malala. **He was taking a huge risk**, but she was right behind him.

Malala and her classmates tried to think of ways they could help, and one of their teachers was especially encouraging. Madam Maryam was clever, and funny, and Malala looked up to her from the moment they met. She was especially impressed that **Madam Maryam had been to college** and, because she earned her own wage, didn't have to rely on a man for support.

Madam Maryam helped the girls to prepare an assembly where they would each deliver a speech about what their school meant to them. Ever since she was tiny, Malala had practiced speeches in front of the mirror and she regularly made presentations to her class. This was a bit different, though. She wouldn't just be speaking to the whole school, there'd be a local TV crew recording everything too!

Moniba gave a beautiful speech, and Malala watched her with admiration. But it was her turn next, and **she trembled with nerves** as she approached the microphone. She knew that she couldn't mess up, not with so many people watching. She took a deep breath and, just like Ziauddin all those years before, as she began to speak, her nerves melted away. In fact, **she found she enjoyed it** so much, she was disappointed when her turn was over!

Even Ziauddin was impressed, and his mind began whirring with possibilities. Before she knew it, he'd arranged for her to speak at a press club—in front of a bunch of journalists!—in Peshawar, the largest city in Swat. But would the journalists listen to an eleven-year-old girl?

Malala arrived to find the club was packed, and even when she realized her speech was being filmed, she wasn't thrown; she just looked straight into the cameras, her eyes blazing, and spoke directly to Fazlullah.

She was too angry to feel scared, but the truth was, in speaking out against Fazlullah and his followers, she was taking a huge risk.

After that, TV and radio journalists lined up to interview her. Journalists were automatically Taliban targets, so they had to be careful what they reported. But Malala was brave enough to say the things they didn't dare say themselves, and they jumped at the chance to quote her.

She brushed off any suggestion that she was putting herself in danger. **The rights of girls were just too important**, and besides, even the Taliban wouldn't stoop low enough to target a child.

Would they?

CHAOS IN MINGORA

Meanwhile, with the army struggling to hold them back, the Taliban bombed a power station and blasted gas pipelines to stop the flow of electricity and gas to people's homes. They even turned off cable TV channels. Now people who had dared to hold on to their TVs had very little to watch.

By the end of 2008, despite the army's efforts, almost all of the enormous district of Swat was now under Taliban control. Even the countryside had become dangerous, and Malala's small house was filling up fast with relatives who had fled their homes. It was cramped and noisy and, with nothing much to do, Malala and Khushal argued constantly.

Meanwhile, outside, death was all around them. It was even creeping into the games that children played. Instead of cops and robbers, there was the army versus the Taliban, and Atal spent a worrying amount of time digging pretend graves in the yard.

Malala longed for peace and quiet but there was literally nowhere to go. After sunset, the people of Swat were **prisoners in their own homes**.

As the dead bodies continued to pile up in Mingora's "Bloody Square," Malala wondered how on earth the Taliban could claim to be "good Muslims" when they kept on killing innocent people. Plenty of people were against Fazlullah, but not many of them were brave enough to say so. Even the deputy commissioner, one of Swat's most senior local officials, was attending Taliban meetings now. **There was no one for people to turn to.**

MALALA EXPLAINS THE FIVE PILLARS OF ISLAM

Muslims are asked to always put our faith first. However, the Holy Qur'an was written in ancient Arabic dialect, so different groups interpret its teachings in different ways, but most Muslims do agree on these five rules:

The Five Pillars of Islam

We are expected to:

⚙ Believe in one God and his prophet Mohammad.

⚙ Pray five times a day, turning to face Mecca, in Saudi Arabia. The Ka'ba inside the Great Mosque there is considered Islam's most holy place.

⚙ Share our wealth with other people who are less fortunate.

⚙ Fast during the holy month of Ramadan, which basically means eating nothing during the day (but having fantastic feasts when it gets dark).

⚙ Make a pilgrimage to Mecca, which is called Hajj, at least once in our lives if we're physically and financially able—1.7 million Muslims made the pilgrimage in 2017!

Where does it say anything about needing the right haircut, or not dancing and listening to music?

MECCA

Are we there yet?

Finally, the day came that Malala had been dreading for months. **Ziauddin's name was read out on Radio Mullah.** Her dad was officially an enemy of the Taliban; Malala was shocked by how scared she felt. Every evening before bed, she double checked the locks on all the doors and gates and prayed to Allah to protect him.

School's Out Forever?

By the end of 2008, the Taliban were everywhere. They now had complete control of almost every district in Pakistan's North-West Frontier Province (which covered a whopping 30,000 square miles [80,000 kilometers]!). And, in December, Fazlullah made his wildest announcement yet.

He has got to be joking!

After January 15, no girl, whether big or little, shall go to school. Otherwise, you know what we can do.

But Fazlullah meant every word.

Malala's class of twenty-seven students had already dwindled to just ten. Now Ziauddin decided he was going to have to close the school altogether.

5   MALALA SPREADS THE WORD

Around the world, the media was noticing what was going on in Pakistan. But while there were plenty of reports on the fighting, only a handful of journalists wrote about the impact the Taliban was having on ordinary people.

However, when news of the school ban reached the BBC, a radio reporter named Abdul Hai Kakar reached out to Malala's dad and asked if any of his students could write for their website. He wanted an **anonymous diary** about life under the Taliban. One brave girl volunteered, but the next day, her dad came storming into school.

I don't want my daughter to be killed!

The other girls were too scared to volunteer. But not Malala. This was her chance to tell the rest of the world what was going on around her.

In the Holy Qur'an it says that "Truth has to come to light, and falsehood has to die." I felt it was my duty as a Muslim to speak up.

The Diary of Gul Makai

First things first—Malala needed a fake name to write under. With the help of Hai Kakar, she decided on "Gul Makai." It means cornflower in Urdu, but it's also the name of a heroine in a Pashtun folk tale, who used the Holy Qur'an to teach men that war is bad. Malala hoped her diary could do the same.

But **she had no idea where to start**. She'd never even kept a personal diary before, and this one was going to be available for everyone to read. Hai Kakar helped by calling and interviewing her each week. He'd write up what she had told him and send it back for Malala to check, before publishing it online.

Malala's first diary entry appeared in early January 2009 under the title "I Am Afraid." Within days, **everyone in Mingora was talking about it** and trying to guess the identity of the schoolgirl author.

A journalist from the *New York Times*—one of the world's largest newspapers—wanted to come to Mingora and make a documentary in the run-up to the school ban. The film would mostly be about Ziauddin as the principal, but the director also asked if Gul Makai could make an appearance. This took things to a whole other level.

Gul Makai's diary was anonymous, but the documentary wouldn't be. Malala knew the risks involved, but **she agreed to it right away**. Here was an even bigger chance to tell the world what was really going on. No way was she passing that up. But by the time the news team arrived, the focus of their documentary had changed completely. Now Malala was the star. The film would follow her for the whole day, from saying her prayers in the morning to brushing her teeth at night! The director wanted everyone to be as natural as they could be.

With the school ban only days away, Malala got upset at one point and began to cry. She was embarrassed at first—thousands of people would see her! But then she realized **it was exactly what they needed to see**: her tears could help people understand just how important education was to girls like her.

> They cannot stop me. I will get my education if it's at home, school, or somewhere else. This is our request to the world—to save our schools, save our Pakistan, save our Swat.

Malala's very last day at school was January 14, 2009, and she and her friends vowed to make it a good one. They played games and sang songs with the younger students and stayed on the school grounds for hours after the bell had rung. But when she got home, she couldn't hold her feelings back any longer and **she sobbed for hours**.

Secret School

With no school to go to, Malala suddenly had a lot of time on her hands, and she didn't want to waste it. She started speaking out against the ban. Over the coming weeks, she made regular trips, with Ziauddin, to Peshawar and other towns and cities that hadn't been taken over by the Taliban yet. She told them exactly what was going on in Swat.

Even though they believed the Taliban would never kill a child, a lot of people were afraid for Malala. Every time she went off to be interviewed, her grandmother would pray to Allah.

Please God, make Malala like Benazir Bhutto, but do not give her Benazir's short life.

Malala didn't have time to be afraid; **she was too busy being angry**. Besides, her hard work was starting to pay off. Thanks to all those appearances on the TV and radio, the people of Pakistan were finally taking notice.

At this point, Fazlullah was hugely powerful in Swat and the North-West Frontier Province in general, but he had far less sway in the rest of the country. If he wanted a chance of winning over those people, he was going to have to give in to mounting pressure (thanks in no small part to Malala and Ziauddin's campaigning) and think again about the ban on girls' education. So, amazingly, less than a month after the ban was introduced, Fazlullah reluctantly agreed that girls up to the age of ten would be allowed to learn again.

Malala and her friends were eleven, but that didn't stop them. She and her classmates swapped their uniforms for plain clothes, hid their school books under their shawls, and practiced what they would say if the Taliban stopped them.

Madam Maryam called it their "silent protest."

Peace in Swat?

Once upon a time in Mingora, gunfire had signalled a celebration—a birth (well, a boy's birth) or a wedding—but the war had changed all that. So when shots rang out in the early hours of February 16, 2009, people were terrified. It was only later that morning that they found out **there was a reason to celebrate**. The Taliban and the local government had settled on a peace deal. The government would impose Sharia law if the Taliban agreed to stop fighting. As part of the deal, older girls could return to school, as long as they covered themselves up in public.

The deal wasn't perfect, but after weeks of bomb blasts and curfews, people were just relieved to return to normality.

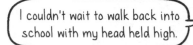

I couldn't wait to walk back into school with my head held high.

Sadly, it soon became obvious that the Taliban wasn't interested in peace at all. And thanks to the deal, their Talibs were officially allowed to patrol the streets and bazaar armed with guns and sticks. One afternoon, when Toor Pekai was shopping, a Talib blocked her path and **threatened to beat her** for not wearing a burqa. Toor Pekai managed to stay calm, even though she was horrified.

By the spring, it was obvious the peace deal had failed. Because they'd complied with the Taliban, the government had basically given up all control, so now **the Talibs could do what-**

How dare they! The burqa has never been part of our Pashtun tradition.

ever they wanted! When the Taliban marched into the nearby district of Buner, the army ordered the local authorities not to fight back. Within days, there were bonfires of TVs and DVDs in the streets.

Pack up your belongings and leave NOW.

In the capi-Islamabad, fear a total Taliban takeover forced government making plans push them out once and for all. In June 2009, after months of careful planning, the army was back, driving through the streets of Mingora.

And there was no mistaking their message: the army wanted civilians out of Mingora because **things were about to get messy**.

6   MALALA ON THE MOVE

Malala had only just been allowed back to school, but now she had to leave, and it was the Taliban's fault yet again! Worst of all, the family would be heading out of Mingora in someone else's car and they could only take absolute essentials with them. Malala was devastated to discover that **she couldn't even bring her schoolbooks**. Upstairs, in desperation, she hid them all in the guest room and prayed they would be safe.

Khushal and Atal were upset too. They were forced to leave their pet chickens behind. So, they gave the birds loads of water and plenty of chicken feed and hoped for the best.

It was the biggest exodus in Pashtun history. With barely any notice, the streets of Mingora were in chaos as families fled their homes, some with just the clothes on their backs and no idea where they were going. But being Pashtun, everyone had faith that the Pashtunwali code of conduct would help them.

Sure enough, Pashtun people in nearby towns threw open their doors and welcomed three quarters of the refugees—**that's over one and a half million people!**—into their homes, schools, and mosques. The rest had no choice but to head for refugee camps where disease was rife and the flimsy tents offered hardly any protection from the blazing summer sun.

TRAFFIC JAM

The journey to Malala's relatives in Shangla usually only took a few hours, but this time the Taliban had blocked so many roads and the traffic was so terrible, that it ended up taking days. The family was aiming to stay with their relatives in the mountains, but **they almost didn't make it** at all. After traveling for three days, they were just a few miles away from their destination when they were stopped at an army checkpoint and told to turn back. At that, Malala's grandmother burst into exhausted tears and begged the soldier to let them pass.

Oh fine, go ahead.

Meanwhile, Ziauddin was heading in the opposite direction, to Peshawar, the capital of their province. Toor Pekai had **begged him not to**, but he was adamant. He wanted to let the authorities and the press know about the terrible conditions they, as internally displaced people (IDPs), were being forced to live under because, as far as he could see, the army was doing hardly anything to help them.

Living in the mountains was challenging:

⚙ Malala opened her suitcase to discover none of the clothes she'd packed matched! She'd been in such a hurry she'd thrown any old thing into her bag.

⚙ While it was good to spend time with her cousins, she missed her books, her friends and the bustle of the city.

⚙ Ziauddin got in touch as often as he could, but phone reception up in the mountains was pretty awful.

⚙ Every night the family gathered around the radio for news of Mingora.

Two Months: Four Moves

As it happened, Malala was about to move even further away. After **six nail-biting weeks**, Ziauddin finally got in touch, and soon after, the family managed to make it to Peshawar to meet him. From there, they traveled to Islamabad to stay with a friend of Ziauddin's. From then on, they had to stay with anyone who would have them, which meant moving again and again.

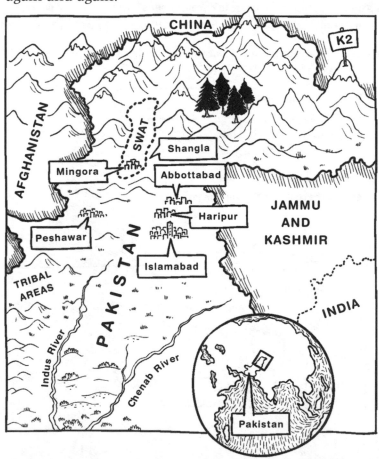

Ziauddin didn't stop campaigning and Malala **stuck right by his side**. They managed to sneak in to a meeting with Richard Holbrooke, the American envoy to Pakistan and Afghanistan. Malala begged him to help girls like her to get an education, but Mr Holbrooke just said, "Your country already has lots of problems," with a dismissive wave of his hand. Girls' education obviously wasn't top of his list. Malala was disappointed, but she quickly bounced back, speaking about the meeting on the radio the next day. The radio station employees were so impressed by her, they offered the family accommodation at a guesthouse they owned in Abbottabad. After so many weeks living in cramped conditions, they jumped at the chance.

Best of all, **Moniba was in Abbottabad too**! Malala couldn't believe her luck. The last time she had seen her best friend, they'd had a fight over something silly. But she didn't need to worry—they quickly made up over cookies and soda and vowed they would never fall out again. For a while, life felt almost normal.

The family stayed in the guesthouse for a week, but then they moved again, to a town called Haripur where an aunt had offered to take them in. Malala knew she was lucky to have a roof over her head, especially when over half a million people were living in sweltering refugee camps, but moving all the time was tiring and she couldn't help longing for home.

Things were so stressful that when Malala's twelfth birthday came around . . .

No one remembered but me! I was upset, of course, but everyone was so stressed that I couldn't make a fuss.

With no cake and no candles to blow out, Malala quietly pictured them in her head. She closed her eyes, blew out the imaginary candles and made a wish—the exact same wish she'd made on her eleventh birthday—for peace in Swat Valley.

MINGORA IN RUINS

Finally, after almost three months away from the valley, an official announcement came: the Taliban had been defeated—it was safe to go home!

On July 24, 2009, the family was back at last. Malala was so excited, but, as they drove through the city, she was filled with disappointment. Mingora looked nothing like she remembered it. **There were bullet holes everywhere**, piles of rubble where buildings once stood, and burned-out vehicles lining the silent and empty streets. Hardly anyone elsc had come home. It seemed they didn't believe Mingora was safe—and who could blame them?

As they drew nearer to their street, everyone fell silent.

Is the house still standing?

Have the soldiers moved in?

What about the chickens?

Malala could barely breathe as her dad opened the gate. Khushal and Atal pushed past her, wading through the overgrown courtyard to check on their beloved chickens. Or what was left of them. **The poor birds had starved to death**. All the boys found were bones and feathers.

Oh, Clucky!

Malala rushed up to the guest room to check on her books. Some of the houses in the street had been looted but thankfully everything at their house was as they left it, even their TV. Malala hugged her books to her chest in relief. But she was still far too upset to feel happy.

Malala and Ziauddin went to check on the school, dreading what they might find there. It was still standing at least, but while they'd been away, the army had moved in. They'd scrawled graffiti on the walls and dropped their cigarette butts all over the floors. They'd also left a letter.

Malala was appalled by the letter and the mess the army had made. These men were supposed to be defending the city and its people, not defacing it and blaming the locals. Their presence was still everywhere: army vehicles clogged up the streets and helicopters buzzed in the sky.

Swat Valley was at peace for now, but **Malala and her family couldn't exactly relax**. The Taliban might have been driven out, but most of its leaders were still free—even Fazlullah. It would only be a matter of time, Malala thought, before they tried to take charge once again.

7 WATCH OUT, MALALA

Over the next few weeks, life slowly began to return to normal. More people came home, the shops reopened, women were allowed to go to the bazaar by themselves again, and music and dancing went on all night. Ziauddin and his friends organized a peace festival in the nearby town of Marghazar as a thank-you to families who had taken people in.

And Malala returned to school. That first day, the classroom buzzed as she and her classmates exchanged stories of where they'd been.

Shortly after that, in August 2009, Malala and her classmates left Mingora once again. Happily this time. They were on a school trip to Islamabad, and they had a blast. They did some sightseeing, went to the theater, and **ate McDonald's for the very first time**! Malala even slipped in a quick TV interview.

Malala had stayed in Islamabad after they were evacuated from Mingora, but this was the first time she was able to really explore the city. The Taliban had set their sights on the capital, but luckily, they hadn't come anywhere near it. So women were free to walk around with their heads completely uncovered—Malala could hardly believe it!

The girls met female doctors and lawyers and activists. Educated women were still in the minority in Islamabad, but the fact that some existed proved to Malala that **her dreams really could come true**. The girls were all so excited on the bus ride home.

MALALA IN CHARGE

Hundreds of children had lost parents in the recent years, so the children's charity UNICEF and an orphanage called the Khpal Kor (My Home) Foundation set up the Child Assembly for the Swat district in an effort to give them a voice. The idea was that young people could be elected to a panel that would listen to the problems of children and young people, then put forward ideas for change.

Early in 2010, the Khushal School was asked to take part. There were sixty places in the assembly and elections to choose a speaker, deputy speaker, and secretary. **Malala was thrilled** to be one of just eleven girls picked to join the panel. Then, at the very first meeting, she was elected speaker.

It felt incredible that young people were finally being taken seriously, and she wasted no time in talking about girls' education to all sorts of important people.

The assembly met every month and passed a number of resolutions about things like:

- ⚙ Rebuilding schools destroyed by the Taliban.

- ⚙ Giving street children the right to education—with no parents to look after them, many more children were now forced to forage in city dumps to survive.

- ⚙ Banning caning as a punishment in schools.

Things seemed to be looking up at last.

CATASTROPHE!

But it wasn't long before **disaster struck again**.

In Summer 2010, when Malala was thirteen, a massive monsoon swept through the valley. The rain was relentless. It forced Malala and her classmates to abandon their lessons for the day and, terrifyingly, they could only get home by **wading through water**!

The problem had been made much worse, though, because the Taliban had chopped down so many trees and sold the wood that they'd left a clear route for the muddy water to come gushing down the mountains, destroying everything in its path.

Roads were washed away and entire villages submerged. The people of Swat couldn't believe it. They seemed to suffer one disaster after another! In fact, this flood turned out to be the **worst ever** in all of Pakistan's history.

No prizes for guessing who were waiting in the wings. Yes, the Taliban were soon back, grabbing the chance to take control again and claiming the floods were a punishment from God.

If the Taliban hadn't chopped down all those trees in the first place, the floods wouldn't have caused so much damage!

Within weeks there was a string of murders and two schools were blown up. The Taliban claimed they were responsible. Malala was so angry. **This wasn't peace!** Technically the war was over and government rule was supposed to have been restored, but the people of Swat were still waiting for that to happen. Until it did, even though they weren't patrolling the streets or dominating the radio airwaves any more, the Taliban were still reigning from the shadows.

Malala had dreamed of becoming a doctor when she grew up, but she was starting to change her mind, because Pakistan was in desperate need of good leaders.

Hmm, maybe I **could** become prime minister one day!

You can have the job! You'd have to be crazy to want to take charge of this mess!

Some Good News

Finally, a ray of light shone through the gloom. In October 2011, a rather exciting email came: **Malala had been nominated for a prize!**

The International Children's Peace Prize is awarded every year to a child whose actions have helped to improve children's rights. Malala was nominated by South African human rights activist, Archbishop Desmond Tutu—one of Ziauddin's heroes!

Malala didn't win the prize, but she did win a lot of new attention, and just a few weeks later, she discovered she'd been awarded Pakistan's very first National Peace Prize for speaking up for girls' education.

In December 2011, Malala traveled to Islamabad and the prime minister, Yusuf Raza Gilani, presented her with the award. She took the opportunity to reel off a long list of concerns, though she wasn't convinced he'd really listen to them.

Together with her classmates, she used the 500,000-rupee (roughly $9,000) prize money to set up an education foundation. The first people she wanted to help were the street children working at the dump.

This was just the start of Malala's campaign, and she didn't want to waste any opportunity that came her way. But Toor Pekai was worried . . .

I don't want awards; I want my daughter. I wouldn't trade a single eyelash of my daughter for the whole world.

WANTED: MALALA

Malala was fourteen when she **flew on a plane for the very first time**. It was January 2012, and she and her family were bound for the city of Karachi where the local government was renaming a girls' school in her honor! Looking up at the sign bearing her name, Malala was at a loss for words. It seemed her message was really getting through.

A few days into the trip, a journalist turned up at the hostel where the family were staying. She'd seen Malala in the *New York Times* documentary and was eager to meet her. They chatted for a while, and then the journalist **dropped a bombshell**.

You seem very positive for someone who's on the Taliban's death list!

What?

Where? Show us!

The journalist brought up the page on her computer, and, sure enough, there was Malala's name alongside another female activist called Shad Begum. Underneath were the words: *These two are spreading secularism and should be killed.*

Reading over her dad's shoulder, Malala felt oddly calm. She was only fourteen—the Taliban couldn't seriously want to kill her. Her parents weren't quite so relaxed, and suggested she stop campaigning for a while. But Malala was adamant. **There was no way she was giving up.**

When they got back to Mingora, they hurried to the police station and discovered that the police had an entire file outlining the danger Malala was in! Now that her message was really spreading, the Taliban wanted to silence her, no matter what.

Welcome to Adulthood

In July 2012, Malala turned fifteen. According to the law, girls become adults at sixteen, and boys at eighteen, but Islam considers girls to be grown-up at fifteen. No longer a child, Malala was old enough to leave school, get married and start a family. Some of her classmates had already done just that. Malala couldn't imagine it! More worryingly, as an adult, she was also now **a legitimate target for the Taliban**.

With Malala in danger, and Ziauddin's name high up on the Taliban's hit list, when one of his friends was shot and injured on his way home from prayers one night, Ziauddin worried that he might be next. From then on, he varied his route to work and spent random evenings sleeping at different friends' houses in order to put the Taliban off the scent.

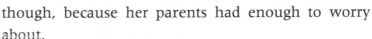

Where shall I stay tonight?

MINGORA

The whole family felt jittery and tense, and Malala started having nightmares. She kept her bad dreams to herself, though, because her parents had enough to worry about.

Just Another Day

October 9, 2012 started out like any other day. Malala tumbled out of bed at the last possible moment. The family ate breakfast before all heading off to school. That's right, all of them. Inspired by Malala's campaign, **Toor Pekai was learning to read and write**, and she had her first lesson arranged that afternoon.

Malala had a Pakistani studies test that morning, and she'd been up late studying. It was one of her worst subjects and she knew she needed to crush it if she was going to be at the top of the class again.

In the end, the test went really well and Malala chatted happily with Moniba as they waited for the bus home and giggled as the driver showed them some magic tricks. Things may have not been perfect in Pakistan, but Malala was determined to not let circumstances bring her down.

Malala's good mood was contagious. As the bus bounced through the streets of Mingora, it was filled with chatter and laughter. Some of the girls even started singing.

The bus climbed the hill, and Malala looked out of the window and frowned. The street was usually packed with people and vehicles, but now it was strangely deserted.

Moments later, the bus braked suddenly, two men climbed onboard . . . and **Malala's life changed forever**.

8 MALALA LOSES A WEEK

One week after the shooting, on October 16, 2012, Malala opened her eyes for the first time.

Lying in an unfamiliar bed, **she had no idea where she was or what had happened** to her. Even now, Malala still doesn't remember anything about it. She's had to rely on her friends, family and doctors to fill in the blanks. It turned out quite a lot had happened to her in the space of a week! Here's how the events unfolded . . .

A RACE AGAINST TIME

The second the bus driver realized Malala had been shot, he sped toward Swat Central Hospital, weaving the packed bus in and out of the busy traffic. In the back, everyone was screaming and crying.

Malala slumped onto my lap and there was blood everywhere. Two other girls had been hit, Shazia and Kainat, but they weren't as badly hurt as Malala.

Moniba

The news of the shooting spread like wildfire across Mingora, and by the time Ziauddin arrived at the hospital, **he had to fight through a crowd of journalists** who'd beaten him there and were lurking around the entrance. Madam Maryam arrived soon after—on the back of her husband's motorcycle!

Swat Central Hospital was small and had only basic medical equipment, so an urgent decision was made to transfer Malala to Peshawar. But this was a four-hour journey by road, and they didn't have the luxury of time, so the army organized a helicopter to get them there as fast as possible. Even so, Ziauddin was terrified the Taliban would catch up with them. Everyone in Mingora knew where Malala was. The Taliban would have no trouble tracking her down; **they might try to shoot her again**.

Meanwhile, by the time Toor Pekai heard the news she was too late for the helicopter ride. Instead, women from all over the neighborhood gathered at the house to comfort her. It was chaos. People were weeping and praying and the phone didn't stop ringing. Then, when Malala's helicopter passed over the house, the women rushed up on to the roof. Toor Pekai joined them and did something very unusual. She took off her scarf and held it up to the sky as if it was an offering to God.

God, I entrust her to you!

FIVE STRESSFUL HOURS

Inside the helicopter, things were not looking good. Malala was vomiting blood and time seemed to be running out. It wasn't until 5 p.m., nearly five hours after Malala had been shot, that they arrived at the Combined Military Hospital in Peshawar. It looked more like a fortress than a hospital.

An alarmingly young-looking doctor named Colonel Junaid greeted them. **The tension was unbearable**, and as he examined Malala, Ziauddin was incredibly anxious . . .

I don't want him operating on my daughter! He barely looks old enough to drive a car!

Relax. I've treated thousands of people like Malala.

Colonel Junaid: Army's top neurosurgeon, expert in gunshot wounds

Quickly, the colonel figured out the bullet that hit Malala was still inside her. It had hit her on her temple, very close to her left eye and then traveled 18 inches (45 centimeters) down through her neck to her shoulder, where it was now lodged. Tiny splinters of bone from her skull were making Malala's brain swell and if they didn't create the space for it to expand, **she would almost certainly die**.

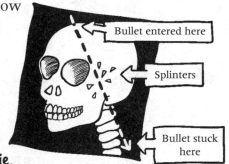

Bullet entered here

Splinters

Bullet stuck here

"We need to operate," Colonel Junaid told Ziauddin shortly before midnight. But the operation was a risky one, and **Ziauddin's hands shook** as he signed the consent papers.

By this time, Toor Pekai had arrived from Mingora with Madam Maryam. The three of them sat outside the operating room and prayed and prayed.

Meanwhile, another surgeon, Dr. Mumtaz, joined the colonel, and together they got to work. They had to be extremely careful, because they were operating close to the part of Malala's brain that controlled speech, and leg and arm movements. One wrong move and **Malala could end up paralyzed**.

Four grueling hours later, the operation was complete. Colonel Junaid wouldn't know it until later, but his decision to operate almost definitely saved Malala's life.

The Taliban Take the Blame

Malala was not out of danger. The pressure on her brain was so immense **she had to be put into a coma** to relieve it and keep her stable.

Meanwhile, the Taliban issued an official statement claiming responsibility for the attack:

She was young but she was promoting Western culture in Pashtun areas . . . Anyone who sides with the government against us will die at our hands. You will see. Other important people will soon become victims.

The message was quite clear: if they were prepared to target a schoolgirl in broad daylight (next to an army checkpoint, in fact), **no one was safe**.

Meanwhile, the people of Pakistan were outraged. Protests were held across the country and large groups gathered to pray for Malala's recovery, lighting candles for her and clutching her picture.

Two Daring Doctors

At around 3 p.m. the day after Malala's operation, two British doctors, Javid Kayani and Fiona Reynolds, arrived at Malala's hospital bedside. By chance, they had been working in nearby Rawalpindi, and they'd been asked to assess Malala before flying home to the UK later that day.

Before they did anything, they turned the taps to wash their hands and were horrified to discover **there was no running water**—in an intensive-care unit!

Dr. Fiona and Dr. Javid grew more and more alarmed as they examined Malala:

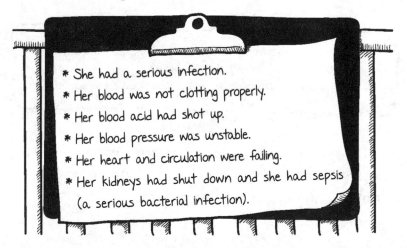

* She had a serious infection.
* Her blood was not clotting properly.
* Her blood acid had shot up.
* Her blood pressure was unstable.
* Her heart and circulation were failing.
* Her kidneys had shut down and she had sepsis (a serious bacterial infection).

Things didn't look good. The operation had been a success, but the poor facilities in the hospital were jeopardizing Malala's recovery. By now, Ziauddin was on the phone to one of Malala's uncles up in Shangla. Between sobs he asked him to **start arranging for Malala's funeral**.

Meanwhile, Dr. Fiona was quietly telling Colonel Junaid that Malala could still survive, but only if she was moved again.

By the end of the day Malala was in another helicopter, bound for the army hospital in Rawalpindi. It had the best facilities Pakistan could offer, but the risk of a terrorist attack was high. There was every chance the Taliban would try to finish the job they'd started. Needless to say, security at the hospital was tight. Soldiers surrounded the perimeter and snipers were stationed on the roof. Inside, Ziauddin and Toor Pekai had their phones confiscated. They couldn't even go to grab a snack without an armed guard!

They didn't argue, though. The Taliban had attacked plenty of well-protected military bases in the past. They could easily find a way to infiltrate the hospital.

Slowly, Malala's condition began to improve, but she was still in a coma and her injures were still severe. If she came through this, she'd need physiotherapy, speech therapy, and more, but **the right facilities just didn't exist** in Pakistan. To stand any chance of recovery, she'd have to be moved again. But where?

By this point, the news of the shooting and Malala's condition had made headlines all over the world. And **the world was outraged.**

People from around the world offered to help. But as Dr. Fiona and Dr. Javid worked at the Queen Elizabeth Hospital in Birmingham, which specializes in treating victims of conflict, it made sense to send Malala to the UK, where they could continue looking after her.

On the Move Again

Getting Malala to Birmingham wasn't as simple as just booking a plane ticket, but luckily for Malala, her story was so well publicized that the ruling family of the United Arab Emirates stepped in to offer **one of their private jets**! Malala couldn't believe it when she found out, later.

This was the first time she'd traveled outside Pakistan, so a passport had to be quickly arranged—it would take a lot longer to organize travel documents for the rest of the family. Ziauddin already had a passport, but he was terrified of leaving his wife and sons behind, because now **the entire family were official Taliban targets**.

In the end, Dr. Fiona agreed to act as Malala's official guardian until the family made it to Birmingham. Letting her go was tough, but at least Malala was heading somewhere safe.

Fiona, we trust you. Please take care of our daughter.

9 Malala Wakes Up

Malala arrived in Birmingham on the afternoon of Monday October 12, 2012.

The following afternoon, her eyes fluttered open for the first time in a week. Everything looked clean and shiny. She was definitely in a hospital, but it couldn't be the tiny one in Swat. Was she even in Pakistan?

A doctor appeared at her bedside and introduced himself as Dr. Javid. Malala was certain she'd never seen him before, but he seemed to know her pretty well. He spoke to her in Urdu, but although Malala knew Urdu better than English, she was so tired and confused that she struggled to understand what he was saying. She tried to ask him where she was, but when she tried to speak, **no sound came out**!

Her whole body felt strange. The hospital lights were too bright and hurt her eyes. She had splitting headaches and was seeing two of everything. She couldn't move her left arm. It was all so uncomfortable and very, very scary.

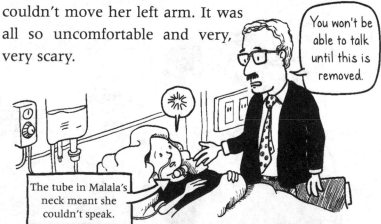

You won't be able to talk until this is removed.

The tube in Malala's neck meant she couldn't speak.

Malala spent the rest of the day drifting in and out of sleep. When she woke up again the next day, she was just as confused. She had tons of questions, but she couldn't speak because of the tube in her throat. Even her hearing was funny—**everything sounded muffled**, like she was underwater.

Dr. Javid gave her a notebook, but her hands were shaking so badly that she couldn't write anything. So Dr. Javid wrote down the alphabet on a piece of paper and asked Malala to spell out words by pointing at the letters. This method worked, but it was excruciatingly slow. She tried to ask a question:

The doctors and nurses explained she was in England and they kept telling her that her family was safe, but **Malala didn't believe them**. If they were safe, why weren't they here with her?

Some Peace of Mind

Malala relaxed a bit when Dr. Fiona showed her a newspaper clipping with a picture of her father, with Atal and her mom in the background. Then, Dr. Javid announced they were going to call her parents. Malala's eyes lit up but, because of her injury, **she wasn't able to smile yet**.

Malala still couldn't speak, but the sound of her dad's voice reassured her, especially when he told her that the family would be joining her as soon as they could.

QUESTIONS

Malala started to feel better. Over the next few days her hands steadied enough for her to write basic questions in her notebook.

She realized that she hadn't seen herself in a mirror in over a week and asked Dr. Fiona if she could take a look. To say she was shocked would be an understatement.

She listened, horrified and fascinated, as Dr. Fiona told her the whole story: the gunmen, the hospitals, the private jet to the UK . . . **Malala didn't remember any of it**. It sounded so ridiculous it was like she was listening to someone else's story!

Then, as reality began to dawn, she grew angry: she hadn't had the chance to give those Talibs a piece of her mind before they'd pulled the trigger!

On Malala's fifth day in Birmingham, the tube was removed from her throat at last. It was a bit croaky, but she had her voice back and, finally, she could actually speak to her parents on the phone.

Come as soon as you can, and don't forget my school bag!

With her memory starting to improve, Malala was eager to get back to her studies. She imagined she'd be flying home in a few weeks, once she was better. And with finals looming, **she needed to study**! But the wait was going to be long and the tests she was worrying about? There was no way she'd be making it back for those.

WAITING

Malala expected her family to join her in two days tops. But the passports took time to get and two days turned into four, then six . . .

Although they spoke on the phone every day, it was an anxious time. It was also incredibly boring. Malala wasn't sleeping very well, so she spent a lot of time just staring at the clock, counting down the minutes until her family walked through the door. The staff did their best to keep her entertained. She played a lot of board games (Connect Four was a favorite) and watched DVDs—but **with an eye-patch** because her vision was still quite blurry.

And she really struggled to cope with the awful hospital food. She longed for her mom's chicken curry. To stop her from going hungry, one of her favorite nurses bought her **bags of cheesy Wotsits (cheese puffs)**. Another brought her Kentucky Fried Chicken that was specially prepared according to Islamic law.

Everyone was so kind to Malala, but she still really missed her family.

FAN MAIL

One day, the head of the hospital's press office came to visit. She had some mail for Malala—a bag stuffed full of cards.

In fact, the cards were from strangers all over the world, many of them schoolchildren. Malala couldn't believe so many people had taken the time to write to her. And when she found out there were over eight thousand more cards and letters in the mail room, she nearly fell out of bed in shock!

Most people wished her a speedy recovery, but some messages were a little strange. One family offered to adopt her. **Someone else proposed marriage!** There were messages from famous people too: Beyoncé and Selena Gomez and Madonna and even Angelina Jolie (who was Malala's favorite actor). After Malala had read them all, her already sore head was spinning!

There were packages too, with toys and boxes of chocolates and teddy bears, but the most precious gift of all was from Benazir Bhutto's two grown-up children. They sent Malala **two shawls** that had once belonged to their mother.

Malala was now so famous that one envelope found its way to her hospital bed simply addressed to:

The cards and presents lifted her spirits, but the very best news of all was that Gordon Brown, former British prime minister and now the United Nations Special Envoy for Global Education, had launched a petition in her honor to demand all children have access to education. Incredibly, it had already gotten a **staggering one million signatures**! Malala was over the moon. It seemed weird, but without the Taliban's actions she'd never have reached so many people.

REUNITED

Eleven days after leaving Pakistan for England, and sixteen days after the shooting, Malala was finally reunited with her family. That may not sound like a very long time, but for Malala, **it had felt like an eternity**.

The moment she heard her parents' voices approach her room, she burst into tears. After all the worry and uncertainty, she was so relieved. She was even happy to see her brothers!

But Ziauddin and Toor Pekai were worried by the way Malala looked and sounded, because **only half of her face was working**. She could speak again, but only in very short, simple sentences.

"The Taliban have snatched my beautiful daughter's smile," Ziauddin cried to Toor Pekai.

Malala tried to reassure them. "I am still Malala," she said.

She'd always been a little vain, but the shooting had changed all that. She was alive, and that was so much more important to her now than how she looked.

The shooting had changed Malala in other ways too. Back in Swat, she was a bit of a cry-baby, weeping over exam results and silly arguments with Moniba. Not anymore! In the hospital, she'd had injections in her neck and staples taken out of her head, and she hadn't cried once. In fact, until her parents walked into her hospital room, **Malala hadn't shed a single tear!**

Facing Reality

After a month in the hospital, the doctors decided they needed to operate on Malala's face. They'd realized that the bullet had severed the facial nerve that controlled the movement on the left side of her face. It affected things like opening her eyes, raising her eyebrows, and smiling. If they didn't operate soon, that side of her face could be **paralyzed forever**.

The operation took over eight hours to complete. And as the surgeon repaired the nerve, he discovered that the bullet had also destroyed Malala's eardrum. No wonder her hearing had been muffled! But he managed to repair that too.

Everything had gone according to plan, but it would be a while before the results of the operation kicked in. In the meantime, Malala had to do exercises in front of the mirror to strengthen her facial muscles.

 They were hard work—and boring! But Malala did them every single day for four months, before she could move her whole face again. It would never quite be the same as it had been before the shooting, but Malala didn't care. Her headaches had finally stopped, and **she could start reading again**! And to mark the occasion, Gordon Brown sent Malala a beautiful edition of *The Wizard of Oz*.

So many people were involved in making me better: surgeons, doctors, nurses, physiotherapists. It's impossible to list everyone.

And there were others who sorted out my transportation and set my family up with a home. I can't thank them all enough. Here are just a few of them:

Dr. Ali Mumtaz

Dr. Fiona Reynolds

Colonel Junaid Khan probably saved my life. My teddy bear is named after him.

Nurse Kat Hackett styled my hair when my head was shaved.

Dr. Javid Kayani was like a second dad to me.

Surgeon Richard Irving operated on my facial nerve and gave me my smile back.

Head of nurses, Julie Tracy was a good friend.

Muslim chaplain, Rehanna Sadiq comforted me with readings from the Holy Qur'an.

Head of the press office, Fiona Alexander kept the press informed—and kept them away from me!

Now What?

As the months rolled by, it became increasingly obvious that Malala and **her family would not be returning to Pakistan**. At least, not yet.

Government officials in Pakistan had offered a million-dollar reward to anyone who handed in Malala's attacker. He'd been identified as a twenty-three-year-old student named Ataullah Khan. So far, he hadn't been caught, but with those who'd hatched the plot against Benazir Bhutto still on the loose, no one felt especially hopeful he'd be arrested any time soon.

> I was disappointed, but I refused to feel angry.

Meanwhile, Fazlullah wasn't the head of the Taliban in Swat any more—he'd risen through the ranks and become the **head of the Taliban in all of Pakistan**! He made it very clear that Malala and Ziauddin were still on his hit list. So, until things changed, Birmingham would be their home.

10 MALALA MOVES OUT

After three long months in the hospital, Malala was finally allowed to leave and join her family in the new home the Pakistani government had arranged for them. The government had agreed to cover all costs for the family's new home.

Buildings in Mingora only have two or three storeys, but this new apartment

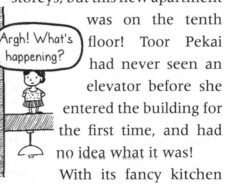

was on the tenth floor! Toor Pekai had never seen an elevator before she entered the building for the first time, and had no idea what it was!

With its fancy kitchen appliances and floor-to-ceiling windows, the apartment was about as different from their home in Mingora as you could get. Malala would spend hours with her nose squished against the glass, watching the people below, and she was often **shocked by what she saw**, especially on Friday and Saturday nights, when girls went out wearing hardly any clothes!

The whole family felt homesick, though. They missed everything from Mingora, even the stench from the stream next to the school!

Once a week, Malala Skyped her old school friends. As their faces filled the screen, Malala held back tears.

"Look," they said. "We're saving you a seat!" It was amazing to be able to see her friends, but **she missed them all so much**, especially Moniba.

No one understands me the way Moniba does.

No Place Like Home

After a little while, the family moved to a new house in a quiet street. By now they had some of their belongings from Mingora with them, and the house was clean and pretty, but it still didn't feel like home.

Khushal hid away in his room playing an Xbox they'd been given.

Atal liked England, especially the Nutella sandwiches.

Toor Pekai missed her friends.

Even Ziauddin was struggling. Some people blamed him for Malala's shooting. They thought he was a **pushy dad** who'd forced his daughter to make speeches and appear on television to make himself seem more important!

Then, one day, he got a phone call from Gordon Brown, and by the time Ziauddin hung up, he was grinning from ear to ear. Gordon had just offered him a job on his United Nations team—Ziauddin would be a Special Advisor on Global Education! **It was the perfect job for him** because he'd get to speak about the importance of education for everyone.

Malala was delighted. She was still desperately homesick, but she was also starting to change her mind about England:

⚙ After so many years of living in fear, it's incredible to walk down the street and not have to worry about being followed or attacked.

⚙ I love that women do all sorts of jobs, from working as a police officer to running massive companies. In England, nothing seems off-limits.

⚙ I like the way people stick to the rules and arrive on time for things.

BACK TO SCHOOL

It was five long months before Malala was finally able to go back to school, and she dressed in her new uniform with a mixture of relief, excitement, and nerves. On the one hand, she couldn't wait to start learning again; on the other **she was terrified** of going to a school full of strangers.

To make matters worse, she was nearly sixteen and she'd been put in a class with fourteen-year-olds to give her more time to prepare for her GCSE exams, which are tests that help determine a student's college and career options. Malala spoke excellent English but the UK curriculum was going to be completely new to her and she'd be starting some subjects from scratch, like music, computer science and home economics.

And Edgbaston High School was nothing like the Khushal School.

Um, understatement of the year!

First of all, it was enormous. For the first few weeks she got hopelessly lost in its maze of corridors and stairwells. Even when she found her way, the classrooms looked totally different than her old school.

Making friends was tough too. The other girls were all very sweet, but spending time with them made Malala miss Moniba and the girls back home even more. Here, she wasn't just plain old Malala either, she was "Malala, the girl who got shot" or "Malala, the activist."

Back in Pakistan, the eight or nine books Malala owned made Malala a total bookworm in the eyes of her friends. Here, she met girls who owned hundreds of books. It was a bit like being in a class full of Malka-e-Noors. Malala worried **she might never be top of the class again**. Still, she was determined to try, and in any case, she had opportunities the other girls could only dream of.

Prizes

In 2013, Malala was nominated for the International Children's Peace Prize for the second time, and this time, to her immense shock and delight, **she won!**

She traveled to Holland for the ceremony, which was her first major trip since leaving the hospital.

She accepted the trophy on behalf of families all over the world whose children were struggling to go to school. As she raised it above her head, she couldn't help thinking about Fazlullah.

Take that, Taliban!

The prize was the first of many. It wasn't long before the shelves in her bedroom were bursting with trophies, medals, and certificates from all over the world.

Then, in the summer, Malala got **a really exciting invitation**—not to a party, but to the United Nations! They wanted her to make a speech in front of their youth assembly on July 12 (her sixteenth birthday!) in New York City.

Only Malala would get excited about having to make a speech on her birthday!

Malala was excited, but a bit apprehensive about the trip. In Pakistan, lots of people think America is a terrible place and that Americans are mean. Most of Malala's ideas about New York came from TV and films. Being in Central Park and Times Square felt like being on a movie set. But the **Americans were nothing like she'd imagined**: they were so friendly and welcoming. She had an amazing time.

On her birthday, Malala woke up with butterflies in her stomach. She spent the morning practicing her speech in front of the mirror. As if speaking to the

United Nations wasn't a big enough deal, she'd been told that **they wanted to name the entire day "Malala Day"** in her honor.

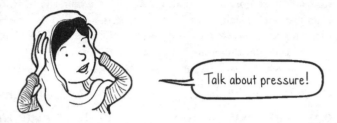

> Talk about pressure!

Feeling nervous but excited, Malala got dressed in her favorite pink shalwar kameez and picked out one of Benazir Bhutto's shawls. She'd never met Benazir, but the second she draped the shawl over her shoulders, she felt calm. It was almost as if Benazir would be with her, every step of the way.

HAPPY BIRTHDAY, MALALA

> Let me say the words the Taliban never wanted her to hear, "Happy sixteenth birthday, Malala."

That's how Gordon Brown (now a good family friend) introduced Malala to the New York assembly. As she stepped up to the podium, her thoughts flashed back to her last birthday. At age fifteen, she'd never even left Pakistan before, and now here she was, about to address over five hundred young people from one of the world's most important organizations, in one of the world's most famous cities.

As Malala stood in front of the microphone a hush fell over the room. **It was a moment to feel proud.** She had achieved so much. She paused briefly, then she began:

Dear brothers and sisters, Malala Day is not my day. Today is the day of every woman, every boy, and every girl who have raised their voice for their rights.

Being shot by the Taliban may have made her famous, but Malala knew she wasn't unique. Thousands of other children around the world still suffered the problems she'd suffered, and she didn't want to let them down. *"I am the same Malala. My ambitions are the same. My hopes are the same. My dreams are the same,"* she said, before delivering the line that would soon become her catchphrase.

One child, one teacher, one book, and one pen can change the world.

Yeah!

Hooray!

There was a pause after she stopped speaking. Then the audience leaped to their feet, clapping and cheering.

As sixteenth birthdays go, it was a pretty extraordinary one. Cards and gifts poured in from people all over the world. Malala even saw her photo projected onto the Brooklyn Bridge. And to cap it all, she got a **birthday message from Beyoncé** on Instagram!

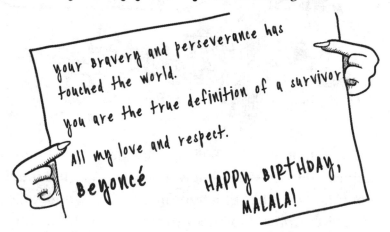

your bravery and perseverance has touched the world.
you are the true definition of a survivor
All my love and respect.
Beyoncé
HAPPY BIRTHDAY, MALALA!

All she'd ever wanted was for the world to hear her message. There was a lot of work still to do, but it finally felt like the **people in power were listening**.

MALALA EXPLAINS MALALA DAY

I really wasn't sure about Malala Day at first, but then I realized, I'd never get a better chance to get my message across.

Now, every year, I try to do something extra special to mark the occasion.

○ On my eighteenth birthday, I opened a school for refugee Syrian girls in Lebanon.

○ On my nineteenth birthday, I launched the #YesAllGirls campaign, asking for twelve years of safe, good-quality education for every single girl on the planet.

○ I spent my twenty-first birthday in Brazil, meeting some of the 1.5 million girls who can't to go to school there because they are too poor, or their world is too violent and racist.

11 WHAT MALALA DID NEXT

The trip to New York was the start of something. A few months later, almost exactly a year after the shooting, on October 8, 2013, her autobiography *I Am Malala* was released. Even though she was still only sixteen and obviously had a lot more of her life to live. She'd co-written it with one of the world's leading foreign correspondents, Christina Lamb.

Now the whole world will know how annoying you are!

Malala was thrilled to be sharing her story, but nervous about strangers reading secret, personal details of her life. In fact, she never imagined quite so many strangers would want to read about her. The book became an instant bestseller, and within three years **1.8 million copies** had sold around the world!

Malala Meets Obama

A few days after the book launch, she was invited to the White House. **President Barack Obama himself** wanted to *"thank her for her inspiring and passionate work on behalf of girls' education in Pakistan."* Wow!

Malala admired the president, so she was incredibly excited to meet him, and she thanked him for supporting girls' education and equality, but she did have some serious matters that she wished to discuss with him as well.

The United States was using missiles carried by drones to attack Taliban targets, but innocent people were being killed.

Malala asked some tough questions, and President Obama clearly took them seriously. He even offered Malala some advice.

The number of famous friends Malala had was growing fast. World-famous soccer star, David Beckham presented her with the Pride of Britain award, and called her *"inspirational"*; Oscar-winning actress Reese Witherspoon found out about Malala through her own teenage daughter and said Malala was: *"an incredible speaker . . . doing incredible things."* Then superstar **Justin Bieber got in touch**:

She's been photographed for magazine covers, appeared in the documentary *He Named Me Malala*, been interviewed by Oprah and David Letterman and written another bestseller, the picture book *Malala's Magic Pencil*—and yes, it was inspired by *Shaka Laka Boom Boom*, the TV show she used to love.

The Big One

In 2014, Malala was nominated for another prize. It was the second time she'd been nominated, in fact, and she really wasn't expecting to win, so when she was called out of chemistry class, Malala assumed she was in trouble. She couldn't believe it when the teacher said, "**You've won!**"

It was just about the biggest prize she could win: the Nobel Peace Prize! Back home that evening, her brothers didn't believe it.

OOooh!

You're at least forty years too young!

They were right! The average age of all the winners in the prize's whole 113-year history was sixty-two— and **Malala was still just seventeen**!

She'd spoken in front of the UN and she'd have to do a speech to accept the Peace Prize too, but when a special school assembly was called to celebrate and Malala had to talk in front of the entire school, she was terrified. To this day, she hasn't got a clue what she said!

Nobel Peace Prize

⚙ Hundreds of people are nominated for Nobel prizes every year. They cover many fields from literature to science, but the Peace Prize is the most famous. Each winner receives a diploma, medal, and certificate, plus a cash prize of around 1.1 million dollars!

⚙ The awards were created by this guy, the fabulously wealthy Swedish inventor and manufacturer, Alfred Nobel. He asked for the awards to be set up after his death.

I love prizes!

⚙ Other winners of the Peace Prize include: Barack Obama, Mother Teresa, Nelson Mandela, and plenty of people you've probably never heard of, who worked away quietly to achieve incredible things.

⚙ Out of 125 winners up to 2014, Malala was only the sixteenth woman.

At seventeen, Malala was the **youngest person ever** to receive the prize, she was the first Pakistani and the very first Pashtun. She shared the award with Kailash Satyarthi (age sixty), who works for children's rights in India.

The award ceremony was in Oslo, Norway, that December, and Malala didn't go alone. She invited Shazia and Kainat, the other two girls who were shot on her bus, and some young female activists she'd met who were also campaigning for girls' education. She had an important point to make.

The speech went viral. It's been viewed on YouTube **millions of times**.

The world was finally taking notice . . . big time!

Juggling

Now that she'd won the biggest prize of all, things were really cooking, and Malala was invited to make speeches all over the world. She had over five thousand requests in just one year! She was so busy, she sometimes didn't get home until one o'clock in the morning. And then **she still had to get herself up for school** just a few hours later—and climbing out of bed in the morning had never been her favorite thing. She struggled to stay awake during lessons and eventually had to slow down the public speaking to get through her GCSEs.

Despite all the distractions, her injuries, her short time in the country, and the new curriculum she'd had to learn, in August 2015 Malala's results came through and she'd **absolutely aced her exams**.

I wonder how Malka-e-Noor would have done.

Malala had been famous for years, but, thanks to the public speaking engagements and fantastic sales of her autobiography, **she'd also become a millionaire**! But she'd never dream of spending all that money on fast cars and fancy houses. She'd already donated her Nobel Prize winnings to rebuild war-damaged schools in Gaza, Palestine, and by 2016, $950,000 of her earnings had been donated to education-based charities around the world.

Naturally there was no way the money would put a stop to Malala's own education. She was soon back at Edgbaston High School. She'd made lots of friends there by now, even though she'd never find another Moniba. And she wasn't worried about being top of the class since she had so much on her plate already! But what would she do when she left school? Obviously, she'd be going to college, but how would she balance all those speaking engagements with studying for a degree?

In the end, she was accepted to study Philosophy, Politics, and Economics (PPE for short) at Oxford University—the perfect choice for anyone wanting to go into politics. Benazir Bhutto had studied at that exact same college. Malala knew it wasn't safe to return to Pakistan yet, but perhaps it wouldn't always be that way . . .

THE MALALA FUND

Malala knew that all the attention she was getting could be put to better use, and, in 2013, she and Ziauddin had set up a fund to help girls across the world who don't go to school—all **130 million of them**! The fund had two aims:

⚙ To find out why girls weren't getting educated.

⚙ To get people who had power to do something about it.

They won support from a charity founded by Hillary Clinton and from the actor Angelina Jolie.

The fund's very first grant was given to an organization in Swat to support the education of forty girls who would otherwise have been forced into work.

GIRL POWER

By Spring 2017, the fund had really taken off, and Malala began her most ambitious project yet: **a six-month trip across four continents**. Her mission? To meet as many girls as possible, listen to their stories, then make sure world leaders knew how to help them.

She called it her Girl Power trip, because:

✪ If all girls went to school for twelve years, poorer countries could add ninety-two billion dollars per year to their economies!

✪ Educated girls are healthier, less likely to marry young, and more likely to have healthy, educated children.

Love school, love the planet!

SCHOOL

✪ One organization reckons that giving girls a secondary education is the best way to invest against climate change. With more girls in school, fewer babies are born and the population doesn't grow so fast. Plus, female leaders often give more priority to climate change than male leaders do.

✪ And, fascinatingly, a country that gives all its children a secondary education, is 50 percent less likely to go to war!

CONFLICT EDUCATION

We ♥ school!

WAR

YES TO EDUCATION

GIRL POWER GOES GLOBAL

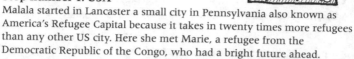

Stop number 1: USA
Malala started in Lancaster a small city in Pennsylvania also known as America's Refugee Capital because it takes in twenty times more refugees than any other US city. Here she met Marie, a refugee from the Democratic Republic of the Congo, who had a bright future ahead.

> I'm off to college to study nursing!

Stop number 2: Canada
Malala spoke to the Canadian parliament and asked them to help find money for global education, especially for refugees.

> *Let future generations say . . . we were the first to live in a world where all girls can learn and lead without fear.*

Stop number 3: Iraq and Kurdistan
On Malala Day, 2017, her twentieth birthday, Malala was at a theme park in Iraq with thirteen-year-old Nayir, who had been forced to flee her home when ISIS terrorists invaded. She lived in a camp and her school was inside a sweltering tent, but she was determined.

> Nothing will keep me from finishing my studies.

Stop number 4: Nigeria
In Lagos, Malala took her friend and activist Amina Yusuf with her to meet the country's acting president. They asked him to improve the standard of education in Nigeria.

> Nigeria is Africa's richest country, but there are more girls out of school here than anywhere else in the world!

I want every girl to have access to education.

Amina is Nigeria's Malala.

Stop number 5: Mexico, Columbia, and Brazil

My first ever visit to Latin America! But I'm saddened by how tough life can be here for girls.

⚙ In Mexico, one in four girls will marry before her eighteenth birthday, 90 percent of them never go back to school.

⚙ In the countryside, girls as young as twelve or thirteen are forced to marry young because they're poor and don't believe they have an alternative.

⚙ The culture is dominated by men, which makes it difficult for girls to follow their dreams.

But there are some very determined girls here too, like Sydney.

There's no children's doctor in my town. I aim to be the first!

Moving On

As she packed for college, Malala hoped she'd done enough to set the wheels of change in motion. Now it was up to world leaders to make sure things happened. But Malala needed to continue her education. She waited until she'd finished her finals to join Twitter because she'd worried that it would distract her from school! But on October 9, 2017, she sent out a special tweet:

Malala

5 years ago, I was shot in an attempt to stop me from speaking out for girls' education. Today, I attend my first lectures at Oxford.

By the end of the day, that tweet had **over one million likes**, thousands of replies, and one extra-special comment:

Khushal

Sorry for being a headache for the last 5 years. So grateful you are still with us. [I know] you miss me but I am coming to Oxford in 2 years.

Coming from Khushal that meant a lot.

Malala loves that her words are now read by so many people and that she can connect with other young people around the world.

Even though she missed her family, Malala settled in at Oxford pretty quickly. She still says that she's a "normal" girl, and it's true that when she's not in class or studying, she'll be listening to Beyoncé or Rihanna, ordering takeout, and hanging out with her friends. **She joined the cricket club**, signed up as a tour guide, and started to learn to drive. She even started writing another book about child refugees, inspired by her own experiences and those of the girls she met on her Girl Power tour.

And of course, she's always busy working with the Malala Fund. But in March 2018, she was finally able to take a very personal trip.

HOME SWEET HOME

Malala had traveled all over the world, but she hadn't yet been back to Pakistan. She sobbed as the airplane touched down in Islamabad.

Everything had been meticulously planned. The army maintained control in Swat Valley, but in other parts of Pakistan, terrorist attacks were happening regularly. Fazlullah was still at large, and Malala and her family were still on his hit list, so they were

heavily guarded and **their itinerary was top secret**. The family traveled by helicopter to Swat. When Malala looked out the window at the mountains and rivers she loved so much, **it was like traveling back in time**. They even landed on the same helipad she'd taken off from, unconscious and dangerously wounded, five and a half years earlier.

Mingora felt busier now, but more peaceful too. Fazlullah's headquarters had been ripped down; fields and trees now stood in its place. The ski resort had re-opened. There was even a new amusement park—the Taliban would not have approved!

As Malala and her family arrived at her old street, they heard a deafening noise. Word of their visit had spread, and **five hundred friends and family members** had gathered to welcome them home. Lots of hugging, praying, and photos followed. Malala, however, searched for just one face in the crowd.

It's so good to see you, Moniba.

Another family was living in their old house, but things hadn't changed much. Malala's books and trophies were still in her old bedroom. But she didn't have time to dwell on them. The trip was only four days long, and soon they had to be back in the car, off to the next engagement. Malala couldn't leave Pakistan without meeting the Pakistani prime minister, Shahid Khaqan Abbasi, and making a speech in parliament. There was still a lot of work to do, but **things in Pakistan were starting to look up**. Since Malala started her fund in 2013, more than six million dollars had been invested in education in Pakistan.

We all join hands for the betterment of Pakistan for our future, to empower our women so they can earn and stand on their own two feet!

The Skeptics

Malala's return trip seemed like a triumph, and most people were absolutely delighted to see her:

> We welcome Malala with open arms!

> Her courage is an example to us all.

> She's my idol.

But not everyone was happy about it:

> Why all the fuss? What has she actually done for our country?

> Yeah, she's just in it for the money and fame.

> I've heard the shooting was staged and that Malala's really a secret agent for the USA!

Malala tried not to let any of this bother her, hoping the results of her mission would speak for themselves.

1,000 TABLETS FOR GIRLS IN RAJANPUR

'Our classrooms are so much better than before!' say the girls of Rajanpur...

EVENING · NEWS

REPAIRING FLOOD-DAMAGED CLASSROOMS IN PUNJAB

Things were changing in other areas of the world too. Malala met the Canadian prime minister, Justin Trudeau, and asked him to promote the importance of girls' education at a meeting of the G7 (the seven most economically advanced countries in the world). In June 2018, Malala received the staggering news that Mr. Trudeau had kept his promise: The G7 countries, the World Bank, and other organizations had **committed a whopping $2.9 billion to girls' education.**

No Let-up

Pakistan will always be home for Malala and her family, but they have managed to find happiness in England for now. Some things have changed: Toor Pekai has begun to learn English and Ziauddin has learned to cook! Other things haven't: Malala still can't get out of bed in the morning, and Khushal and Atal continue to drive her up the wall when she visits! But no one in the family is sure they'll ever get used to the rain in England.

No wonder so many people shop online.

Then, in June 2018, Malala received the news that **Fazlullah had been killed** by an American drone strike. Maybe she'd be able to return to Pakistan sooner than she'd thought? She didn't celebrate, though; she knew his death wouldn't mark the end of terrorism in Pakistan.

Malala isn't quite sure what she wants to do when she finishes at Oxford.

Maybe the answer lies in what she's already doing: finding more young women who will rise up and make their voices heard. She's met so many. Here are just a few of them:

In northern India, Zainab refused prize money for being a brilliant student, and asked for a school in her village instead.

In Iraq, Tahany risked her life to save books from the library, when ISIS terrorists tried to burn it down.

In Guatemala, Emelin campaigned for months to get better education and healthcare for girls in her village.

In Nigeria, Peace founded an organization to encourage parents to send their daughters to school.

In Nepal, Gaurika used prize money from swimming competitions to raise awareness about girls who couldn't go to school.

And I can't wait to see what these remarkable girls achieve next. Maybe one day there really might be education for all!

She was the youngest competitor in the Rio Olympics when she was just thirteen!

OK, Malala, maybe you do know what you're talking about!

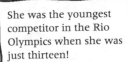

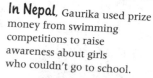

TIMELINE

Phew! I have been busy!

July 12, 1997
Malala is born.

October 7, 2001
The Unitied States invades Afghanistan, driving many Taliban leaders into Pakistan.

| 1995

| 2006

| 2007

January 12, 2002
Fazlullah becomes leader of TNSM.

July 12, 2007
Fazlullah declares war on the Pakistani government.

December 27, 2007
Girls' schools in
Pakistan are targeted
by the Taliban.

June 2009
Malala's family is
evacuated from
Mingora.

July 24, 2009
Malala and her family
return home to
Mingora.

| 2008 | 2009 | 2010

January 3, 2009
Malala's first
anonymous diary entry
is posted to the BBC
Urdu blog.

January 15, 2009
The Taliban bans school
for girls in Pakistan.

Schools for girls are
forbidden by Islam.

February 16, 2009
A peace deal is
agreed between the
government and the
Taliban, but the peace
soon fails.

2010
Malala is elected
speaker of the Khpal
Kor Foundation Child
Assembly for the Swat
district.

December 19, 2011
Malala is awarded
Pakistan's first National
Peace Prize.

| 2010

| 2011

January 2012
Malala discovers she's on
the Taliban's wanted list.

October 9, 2012
Malala is shot on the bus coming home from school. She is rushed to hospital, then airlifted to Peshawar where surgeons operate to save her life.

October 10, 2012
Malala is transferred by helicopter to hospital in Rawalpindi, then by private jet to the UK.

October 12, 2012
Malala arrives in Birmingham, UK.

October 16, 2012
Malala wakes up in the hospital.

2012 | 2013

January 3, 2013
Malala is discharged from the hospital and moves into a new home in the UK.

February 4, 2013
Malala and Ziauddin set up the Malala Fund to help girls around the world get an education.

July 12, 2013

Malala makes a speech at the UN Youth Assembly in New York, delivering her famous line: "One child, one teacher, one book, and one pen can change the world."

September 6, 2013

Malala is awarded the International Children's Peace Prize in Holland.

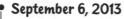 **2014**   **2015**

October 8, 2013

Malala's autobiography, *I Am Malala*, is released. President Barack Obama invites her to meet him.

July 12, 2014

On Malala's eighteenth birthday, she opens a school for refugee Syrian girls in Lebanon.

• October 10, 2014

Malala is awarded the Nobel Peace Prize. She donates the prize money to help rebuild war-damaged schools in Gaza, Palestine.

• April 11, 2017

Malala begins her Girl Power world tour to campaign for girls' rights to education.

• October 9, 2017

Malala attends her first lectures at Oxford University.

| 2016

| 2017

| 2018

• March 31, 2018

Malala visits Pakistan for the first time since her shooting.

• June 7, 2018

G7 countries, the World Bank, and other organizations commit $2.9 billion to girls' education.

Glossary

activist: A person who campaigns to raise awareness of a problem in order to encourage political or social change.

burqa: An item of clothing worn by some Muslim women to cover the whole body and face.

Gul Makai: The heroine of a Pashtun folk tale and the name Malala used to publish her diary entries on BBC Urdu.

henna: Dye used to create temporary tattoos.

internally displaced persons (IDPs): People who have been forced to leave their homes, but stay within their own country.

Islamabad: Pakistan's capital city.

Khegara/Shegara: Part of the Pashtunwali code of conduct that encourages respect for other people, animals and the environment.

Khushal Khan Khattak: A legendary poet of the 1600s. Ziauddin named the Khushal School after him.

madrasa: A religious school that teaches its students about Islam.

Malalai of Maiwand: A teenage warrior from the 1800s. Malala was named after her.

melmastia: The concept of hospitality and part of the Pashtunwali code of conduct.

Mingora: The city in Pakistan where Malala was born.

niqab: A scarf that covers a woman's head and most of her face.

Nyaw aw Badal: The concept of justice and revenge according to the Pashtunwali code of conduct.

Pashto: The language spoken by Pashtun people.

Pashtun: A tribe based in Pakistan and Afghanistan.

Pashtunwali: A code of conduct followed by Pashtuns.

148

purdah: Meaning veil or screen, a Muslim woman "observes Purdah" when she covers her face, and sometimes her whole body, in public.

Radio Mullah: Maulana Fazlullah's illegal radio show that helped him to spread his extremist ideas in Pakistan.

refugee: Someone who is forced to leave their home to escape a war or natural disaster.

Sabat: The concept of loyalty and part of the Pashtunwali code of conduct.

secularism: The belief that religion should not have any influence over the way a government is run.

shalwar kameez: Trousers and tunic typically worn by people from South Asia.

Sharia law: A code that shows Muslims how to live their lives. It can be interpreted in different ways.

shuttlecock burqa: A burqa with a mesh screen covering the wearer's eyes.

Swat Valley: A beautiful part of Pakistan, sometimes called the Switzerland of Asia. Mingora (where Malala grew up) is one of Swat's biggest cities.

Swat Qaumi Jirga: An assembly set up to challenge Fazlullah's and the TNSM's views.

Taliban: A violent Islamic group that interprets Muslim Sharia law in extreme ways and with severe punishments.

Talibs: Members of the Taliban.

Tehrik-e-Nifaz-e-Shariat-e-Mohammadi (TNSM): A Pakistani militant group aiming to enforce Sharia law.

Tehrik-i-Taliban Pakistan: The Taliban Movement of Pakistan.

United Nations: An international organization, set up by the governments of several countries to encourage and maintain world peace and security.

Urdu: The official national language of Pakistan.

Notes

27   "shall not . . . the home": Qur'an 24:31.

47   "Sir, . . . cry for you": Malala Yousafzai and Christina Lamb, *I Am Malala*, New York: Little, Brown and Company, 2013; page 100.

56   "We will defeat . . . extremism!": Malala Yousafzai and Patricia McCormick, *I Am Malala* (Young Readers Edition), New York: Little Brown Books for Young Readers, 2016; page 55.

59   "If you stay . . . to exist": Catherine Shoard, *"He Named Me Malala* Review: Awed Documentary Captures Extraordinary Subject." *Guardian*, September 4, 2015. See theguardian.com/film/2015/sep/04/i-am-malala-review-awed-documentary-captures-extraordinary-subject.

61   "How dare . . . from learning": Yousafzai and Lamb, *I Am Malala*; page 100.

68   "They cannot . . . our Swat": Yousafzai and Lamb, *I Am Malala*; page 135.

88   "These two . . . be killed": Yousafzai and Lamb, *I Am Malala*; page 211.

95   "She was young . . . become victims": Yousafzai and Lamb, *I Am Malala*; page 216.

118   "Let me say . . . Malala'": Gordon Brown, "UK's Brown praises Malala, wishes her 'happy birthday,'" *NBC News* video, 0:36, July 12, 2013. See nbcnews.com/video/uks-brown-praises-malala-wishes-her-happy-birthday-36994627531.

119   "Dear brothers and sisters . . . their rights"; "I am the same . . . are the same": Yousafzai and McCormick, *I Am Malala*; pages 195–96.

120   "One child . . . the world": Yousafzai and McCormick, *I Am Malala* (Young Readers Edition), pages 195–96.

120   "Your bravery . . . Malala!": Andrew Gruttadaro, "Beyonce Posts Heartwarming Message for Malala Yousafzai's 16th Birthday." *Hollywood Reporter*, July 13, 2013. See hollywoodlife.com/2013/07/13/beyonce-malala-yousafzai-birthday-message-pic.

123 "thank her . . . in Pakistan": Becky Bratu, "Pakistani girl Malala Yousafzai meets Obamas at White House." *NBC News*, October 11, 2013. See nbcnews.com/news/world/pakistani-girl-malala-yousafzai-meets-obamas-white-house-flna8C11382026.

123 "Don't join . . . turn gray!": Susan McPherson, "Malala Yousafzai: Wise Beyond Her Years, But Still a Teenager." *Medium*, August 24, 2014. See medium.com/thelist/malala-yousafzai-wise-beyond-her-years-but-still-a-teenager-887db3d06ea8.

124 "inspirational": Jodi Guglielmi, "David Beckham Calls Malala Yousafzai a 'True Role Model' While Meeting Her for the Second Time." *People*, September 28, 2015. See people.com/celebrity/david-beckham-calls-malala-yousafzai-a-true-role-model.

124 "an incredible . . . incredible things": Jenelle Riley, "Reese Witherspoon Bolsters Education for Girls with Malala Fund." *Variety*, October 7, 2014. See variety.com/2014/film/features/reese-witherspoon-malala-fund-focuses-on-education-for-girls-1201323104.

127 "I tell . . . want change": Malala Yousafzai, Nobel Lecture for the Nobel Prize (speech in Oslo, Norway; December 10, 2014). See nobelprize.org/prizes/peace/2014/yousafzai/26074-malala-yousafzai-nobel-lecture-2014.

132 "Let future . . . without fear": Malala Yousafzai, Nobel Lecture, 2014.

134 "5 years ago . . . at Oxford": Malala Yousafzai, Twitter post, October 9, 2017, 8:39 am, see twitter.com/malala/status/917414203186667520?lang=en.

134 "Sorry for being . . . 2 years": Khushal Yousafzai, Twitter post, October 9, 2017, 9:28 a.m. See twitter.com/KhushalYusafzai/status/917426665101381632.

137 "We all . . . two feet!": Mohammad Zubair Khan, "Malala Yousafzai returns to Pakistan in 'dream' trip to push education for girls." *The Telegraph*, March 29, 2018. See telegraph.co.uk/news/2018/03/28/malala-yousafzai-returns-pakistan-first-time-since-taliban-attack.

Bibliography

Bratu, Becky. "Pakistani girl Malala Yousafzai meets Obamas at White House." *NBC News*, October 11, 2013. See nbcnews.com/news/world/pakistani-girl-malala-yousafzai-meets-obamas-white-house-flna8C11382026.

Brown, Gordon. "UK's Brown praises Malala, wishes her 'happy birthday.'" *NBC News* video, 0:36. July 12, 2013. See nbcnews.com/video/uks-brown-praises-malala-wishes-her-happy-birthday-36994627531.

Gruttadaro, Andrew. "Beyonce Posts Heartwarming Message for Malala Yousafzai's 16th Birthday." *Hollywood Reporter*, July 13, 2013. See hollywoodlife.com/2013/07/13/beyonce-malala-yousafzai-birthday-message-pic.

Guglielmi, Jodi. "David Beckham Calls Malala Yousafzai a 'True Role Model' While Meeting Her for the Second Time." *People*, September 28, 2015. See people.com/celebrity/david-beckham-calls-malala-yousafzai-a-true-role-model.

Khan, Mohammad Zubair. "Malala Yousafzai returns to Pakistan in 'dream' trip to push education for girls." *Telegraph*, March 29, 2018. See telegraph.co.uk/news/2018/03/28/malala-yousafzai-returns-pakistan-first-time-since-taliban-attack.

Malala Fund, 2018. See malala.org.

McPherson, Susan. "Malala Yousafzai: Wise Beyond Her Years, But Still a Teenager." *Medium*, August 24, 2014. See medium.com/thelist/malala-yousafzai-wise-beyond-her-years-but-still-a-teenager-887db3d06ea8.

Riley, Jenelle. "Reese Witherspoon Bolsters Education for Girls with Malala Fund." *Variety*, October 7, 2014. See variety.com/2014/film/features/reese-witherspoon-malala-fund-focuses-on-education-for-girls-1201323104.

Shoard, Catherine. "*He Named Me Malala* Review: Awed Documentary Captures Extraordinary Subject." *Guardian*, September 4, 2015. See theguardian.com/film/2015/sep/04/i-am-malala-review-awed-documentary-captures-extraordinary-subject.

Yousafzai, Khushal. Twitter post. October 9, 2017, 9:28 a.m. See twitter. com/KhushalYusafzai/status/917426665101381632.

Yousafzai, Malala. Nobel Lecture. Speech for the Nobel Prize, Oslo, Norway; December 10, 2014. See nobelprize.org/prizes/peace/2014/yousafzai/26074-malala-yousafzai-nobel-lecture-2014.

———. Twitter post. October 9, 2017, 8:39 am. See twitter.com/malala/status/917414203186667520?lang=en.

Yousafzai, Malala and Christina Lamb. *I Am Malala: The Girl Who Stood Up for Education and Was Shot by the Taliban*. New York: Little Brown and Company, 2013.

Yousafzai, Malala and Patricia McCormick. *I Am Malala: How One Girl Stood Up for Education and Changed the World* (Young Readers Edition). New York: Little Brown Books for Young Readers, 2016.

INDEX

Use these pages for a quick reference!

About the Author

Lisa Williamson is an award-winning, bestselling author. She studied drama at Middlesex University and has acted on both stage and screen. She lives in England.

About the Illustrator

Mike Smith is the author and illustrator of a number of children's books and the winner of the Macmillan Prize for children's book illustration. He lives in Cambridge, England.